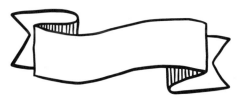

A CULINARY JOURNEY THROUGH ARMENIA'S HEART AND SOUL
DEDICATED TO MY GRANDMOTHER OLGA

Overview of Armenia's Cuisine
A Culinary Tapestry Unveiled

Nestled in the South Caucasus, Armenia boasts a rich culinary heritage shaped by its mountainous terrain, diverse microclimates, and millennia of history. This book invites you to explore the vibrant world of Armenian cuisine, where ancient traditions meet modern innovations.

Armenian food is deeply rooted in the rhythm of seasons and family gatherings. Meals are social affairs, with tables laden with an array of dishes meant for sharing. This custom, known as "**sufra**," reflects the warm hospitality ingrained in Armenian culture.

The country's cuisine is characterized by the use of fresh, locally-sourced ingredients. Staples include:

- Lavash: A soft, thin flatbread integral to every meal
- Herbs: Tarragon, cilantro, basil, and parsley feature prominently
- Vegetables: Eggplant, tomatoes, peppers, and leafy greens
- Grains: Wheat, barley, and bulgur form the foundation of many dishes
- Fruits: Apricots, pomegranates, and grapes are celebrated in both fresh and dried forms
- Nuts: Walnuts and almonds add texture and depth to various recipes
- Yogurt and cheese: Integral components in both savory and sweet preparations

As we journey through Armenia's diverse regions, from the fertile Ararat Valley to the shores of Lake Sevan, we'll uncover unique local specialties and time-honored cooking techniques. We'll explore the art of dolma-making, the secrets behind the perfect khorovats (Armenian barbecue), and the intricate spice blends that give Armenian cuisine its distinctive flavor profile.

Join us as we delve into the heart of Armenian gastronomy, where every dish tells a story of resilience, creativity, and the enduring power of culinary tradition.

Armenian Dining Etiquette

- **Hospitality:** Armenians are known for their generous hospitality. Refusing an invitation or food can be considered impolite. If you're full, it's better to accept a small portion and eat slowly.
- **Arrival:** Guests often bring a small gift, such as flowers, chocolates, or a bottle of cognac. Remove your shoes when entering someone's home unless the host insists otherwise.
- **Seating:** Wait to be seated. The most honored guest is usually seated farthest from the door.
- **Starting the meal:** The meal begins when the host says "Bari akhorjak" (Enjoy your meal). It's polite to wait for this cue.
- Serving: Hosts typically serve guests. It's courteous to accept at least a small portion of everything offered.
- **Using utensils:** While forks and spoons are common, many dishes are eaten with lavash bread used to scoop up food.
- **Pace:** Meals are leisurely affairs. Eat slowly and engage in conversation.
- **Toasting:** Toast-making is an important ritual, often led by a tamada (toastmaster). Each toast can be quite elaborate. It's customary to maintain eye contact during toasts.
- **Drinking**: Never pour your own drink. Wait for others to pour for you, and reciprocate the gesture.
- **Finishing:** Leaving a clean plate signals you're still hungry. Leave a small amount of food to indicate you're satisfied.
- **After the meal:** Offer to help clean up, but don't be surprised if your offer is politely refused.
- **Leaving**: Don't rush to leave after a meal. Lingering for conversation is expected and appreciated.
- **Reciprocation:** If you've been invited to someone's home, it's customary to reciprocate the invitation in the future.

Table of Contents

A culinary journey

ARARAT VALLEY REGION

Mains and apps:
1. Khorovats
2. Losh Kebabs
3. Chamatov Keufteh (Armenian Cumin Fingers)
4. Armenian Lavash
5. Lahmajun (Flatbread with Spiced Lamb)
6. Stuffed Tomatoes
7. Eggplant Dolma
8. Ganach Lupia (Tomato-Braised Green Beans)
9. Plov with Pumpkin
10. Armenian Rice Pilaf
11. Sini Manti (Armenian Baked Dumplings)
12. Harissa (Wheat and Meat Porridge)

Soups & Salads
1. Shepherd's Salad
2. Cabbage salad
3. Havabour Soup (Chicken and Wheat Soup)
4. Eetch (Bulgur and Tomato Dish)
5. Tourshi (Armenian Pickled Vegetables)
6. Canned Tomatoes

Spreads, Jams and Condiments
1. Azerbaijani Seasoning

Desserts:
1. Gata (Armenian Sweet Pastry)
2. Tarragon Lemonade
3. Baked apple
4. Apricot Preserves
5. Choreg (Armenian Easter Bread)
6. "Gift" Cake (Tort "Nver")

Table of Contents
A culinary journey

LAKE SEVAN REGION

Mains and apps:
1. Khorovats
2. Losh Kebabs
3. Chamatov Keufteh (Armenian Cumin Fingers)
4. Armenian Lavash
5. Lahmajun (Flatbread with Spiced Lamb)
6. Stuffed Tomatoes
7. Eggplant Dolma
8. Ganach Lupia (Tomato-Braised Green Beans)
9. Plov with Pumpkin
10. Armenian Rice Pilaf
11. Sini Manti (Armenian Baked Dumplings)
12. Harissa (Wheat and Meat Porridge)

Soups & Salads
1. Shepherd's Salad
2. Cabbage salad
3. Havabour Soup (Chicken and Wheat Soup)
4. Eetch (Bulgur and Tomato Dish)
5. Tourshi (Armenian Pickled Vegetables)
6. Canned Tomatoes

Desserts:
1. T'tu Lavash (Armenian Sour Fruit Rollups)
2. Pakhlava
3. Armenian Ponchik (Filled Doughnuts)

Table of Contents
A culinary journey

SYUNIK-VAYOTS DZOR REGION

Mains and apps:

Soups & Salads

Desserts:

Table of Contents
A culinary journey

LORI-SHIRAK REGION

Mains and apps:
1. Zhingalov Khats Herb-Filled Flatbread
2. Basterma with Eggs
3. Kerusous (Armenian One-Pot Meal)
4. Lamb Stew with Tarragon
5. Pasuts Tolma
6. Baked Zucchini Halves
7. Pomegranate Seeds Pilaf
8. Roast Goose with Apricots in Wine
9. Pamidorov Dzvadzegh (Creamy Armenian Scrambled Eggs with Tomatoes)
10. Crispy Cabbage Cutlets
11. Open-Faced Meat Pie with Potato Crust

Soups & Salads
1. Gelorig Meatball Soup
2. Khashlama
3. Tomato and Bulgur Soup
4. Tabbouleh
5. Spanakhov Asoudi
6. Armenian Kelekyosh (Lentil and Yogurt Soup)

Desserts:
1. Fruit Compote
2. Sweet sujuk
3. Honey Cookies
4. Honey Cake
5. Crumb cake
6. Crumb cake

Overview of Armenia's Regions:
A Culinary Tapestry Unveiled

In this remarkable cookbook, we embark on a gastronomic voyage through the diverse regions of Armenia, uncovering the unique flavors and culinary traditions that define each area.

To make it easier to represent the culinary specialties without repeating recipes , he book is thoughtfully organized in regional major sections, allowing readers to explore the distinct culinary tapestry that weaves together the various corners of this enchanting country.

Ararat Valley Region

This fertile region, including Yerevan, is known for:
- Abundance of fresh fruits and vegetables
- Apricots (Armenia's national fruit) feature prominently
- Specialties: Yerevan-style kyufta (spiced meatballs), ghapama (stuffed pumpkin)
- Wine production, especially in Areni
- Influence of urban cuisine and modern culinary trends

Lake Sevan Region

Centered around Armenia's largest lake, this region is characterized by:
- Fresh fish dishes, especially ishkhan (Sevan trout)
- Crayfish preparations
- Herbs gathered from surrounding mountains
- Specialties: Sevan khash (fish soup), smoked fish

Syunik-Vayots Dzor Region

This southern region is known for:
- Hearty meat dishes, especially lamb and goat
- Unique cheeses like motal (goat cheese aged in a sheepskin)
- Wild herbs and mushrooms foraged from forests
- Specialties: Syunik-style tolma (stuffed grape leaves), zhengyalov hats (bread stuffed with herbs)

Lori-Shirak Region:

This northern region's cuisine is influenced by its cooler climate:
- Emphasis on preserved foods and hearty stews
- Extensive use of grains like wheat and barley
- Specialties: Khash (cow's feet soup), Lori-style khorovats (barbecue)
- Unique dairy products like tan (fermented milk drink)
- Influence of Georgian cuisine due to proximity

Ararat Valley Region

Khorovats

Grilled Meat Skewers

 10 servings   90 minutes

INGREDIENTS

- 1.5 lbs lamb or beef, cubed
- 1 large onion, finely chopped
- 3 cloves garlic, minced
- 1/4 cup vegetable oil
- Juice of 1 lemon
- 1 teaspoon ground cumin
- 1 teaspoon paprika
- Salt and pepper to taste
- Fresh herbs for garnish (mint or cilantro)
- Wooden skewers, soaked in water

DIRECTIONS

1. Prepare Marinade (10 minutes):
- In a bowl, mix chopped onions, minced garlic, vegetable oil, lemon juice, cumin, paprika, salt, and pepper.
2. Marinate Meat (1 hour):
- Add the cubed meat to the marinade, ensuring each piece is well-coated. Cover and refrigerate for at least 1 hour to let the flavors infuse.
3. Skewer Meat (15 minutes):
- Thread the marinated meat onto the soaked wooden skewers, ensuring an even distribution.
4. Grill (20-30 minutes):
- Preheat the grill to medium-high heat. Grill the skewers for 10-15 minutes per side or until the meat is cooked to your liking.
5. Baste (10 minutes):
- Occasionally baste the kebabs with any remaining marinade during grilling for added flavor.
6. Garnish (5 minutes):
- Once done, remove the kebabs from the grill. Garnish with fresh herbs.
7. Serve (10 minutes):
- Serve hot with your favorite accompaniments, such as flatbread, rice, or a refreshing salad.

Losh Kebabs

 10 servings   90 minutes

INGREDIENTS

- 1 lb ground lamb (or a mix of lamb and beef)
- 1/2 medium onion, very finely minced (about 1/2 cup)
- 2 cloves garlic, minced (about 1 teaspoon)
- 1/4 cup finely chopped parsley
- 1 tablespoon mild red pepper paste
- 1 teaspoon salt
- 1/2 teaspoon black pepper
- 1/4 teaspoon ground allspice
- 1 tablespoon tomato paste
- 1 large egg (optional, for binding)

DIRECTIONS

1. In a large bowl, combine all ingredients. Mix thoroughly but gently to avoid overworking the meat.
2. Cover and refrigerate for at least 1 hour to allow flavors to meld.
3. Divide the mixture into 8 equal portions (about 2 oz each) and shape into oval patties, about 1/2 inch thick.
4. Preheat your grill to medium-high heat (about 400°F).
5. Grill the patties for about 4-5 minutes per side, or until they reach an internal temperature of 160°F for medium.
6. Let rest for 3-5 minutes before serving.

Chamatov Keufteh (Armenian Cumin Fingers)

 4 servings   30 minutes

INGREDIENTS

- 1 lb ground lamb (or beef)
- 1/2 cup fine bulgur wheat
- 1 small onion, very finely minced
- 2 cloves garlic, minced
- 1/4 cup finely chopped parsley
- 2 tbsp tomato paste
- 2 tbsp cumin seeds, toasted and ground
- 1 tsp paprika
- 1 tsp Aleppo pepper (or 1/2 tsp red pepper flakes)
- 1 tsp salt
- 1/2 tsp black pepper
- 1/4 cup ice water

For serving:
- Lavash bread or pita
- Sliced onions
- Chopped parsley
- Lemon wedges

DIRECTIONS

1. Soak the bulgur in warm water for 15 minutes, then drain well.
2. In a large bowl, combine the ground meat, soaked bulgur, minced onion, garlic, parsley, tomato paste, ground cumin, paprika, Aleppo pepper, salt, and black pepper.
3. Gradually add ice water while kneading the mixture by hand for about 5-7 minutes until it becomes sticky and well-combined.
4. Cover and refrigerate for at least 1 hour to allow flavors to meld.
5. Preheat your grill or broiler.
6. Wet your hands with cold water and shape the mixture into finger-like kebabs, about 3 inches long and 1 inch thick.
7. Grill or broil the kebabs for about 3-4 minutes per side, until browned and cooked through.
8. Serve hot with lavash or pita bread, sliced onions, chopped parsley, and lemon wedges.

These Chamatov Keufteh are known for their distinctive cumin flavor, which sets them apart from other Armenian kebabs. The combination of ground meat and bulgur gives them a unique texture, while the spices provide a warm, aromatic taste. They're perfect for grilling and make a delicious main course or appetizer.

Armenian Lavash

🍴 2 servings   🕐 15 minutes

INGREDIENTS

- 4 cups all-purpose flour
- 1 1/2 cups warm water
- 1 tsp salt
- 1/2 cup sourdough starter

Lavash can be served as a wrap, used to scoop up dips and salads, or simply enjoyed on its own. It's a versatile bread that's an integral part of Armenian cuisine and widely enjoyed throughout Western Asia and the Caucasus.

DIRECTIONS

1. Prepare the dough:
   - In a large bowl, mix flour and salt.
   - Add the sourdough starter and warm water.
   - Knead the dough for about 10 minutes until smooth and elastic.
   - Cover the bowl with a damp cloth and let it rise in a warm place for 2-3 hours.
2. Shape the lavash:
   - After the dough has risen, divide it into 8-10 small portions.
   - On a floured surface, roll each portion into a very thin oval or circle, about 1/8 inch thick.
3. Cook the lavash:
   - Traditionally, lavash is cooked in a tonir (clay oven). For home cooking, use a very hot cast-iron skillet or griddle.
   - Place the rolled-out dough on the hot surface.
   - Cook for about 1 minute on each side, or until light brown spots appear.
   - The bread should puff up slightly while cooking.
4. Cool and store:
   - Remove from heat and let cool on a wire rack.
   - Once cooled, stack the lavash and store in a plastic bag to keep soft.

Notes:
- Lavash is best eaten fresh but can be stored for several days.
- To reheat, sprinkle with water and warm in the oven for a few minutes.
- Thickness and shape may vary depending on regional preferences.

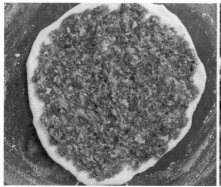

Lahmajun (Flatbread with Spiced Lamb)

 2 servings 30 min

INGREDIENTS

For the dough:

- 3 cups all-purpose flour
- 1 tsp salt
- 1 tsp sugar
- 1 tsp active dry yeast
- 1 cup warm water
- 2 tbsp olive oil

For the topping:

- 1 lb ground lamb (or beef)
- 1 onion, finely minced
- 3 cloves garlic, minced
- 1/4 cup tomato paste
- 2 tbsp red pepper paste
- 1/4 cup finely chopped parsley
- 1 red bell pepper, finely minced
- 1 tsp ground cumin
- 1 tsp paprika
- 1/2 tsp allspice
- Salt and black pepper to taste

DIRECTIONS

1. For the dough: Mix flour, salt, sugar, and yeast. Add warm water and olive oil, knead until smooth. Let rise for 1 hour.
2. For the topping: Mix all ingredients thoroughly. Process in a food processor until it forms a smooth paste. Drain excess liquid.
3. Preheat oven to 450°F (230°C) with a baking stone or inverted baking sheet inside.
4. Divide dough into 8 pieces. Roll each very thin, about 1/8 inch thick.
5. Spread a thin layer of meat mixture on each flatbread, leaving a small border.
6. Bake for 8-10 minutes until edges are crisp and meat is cooked.
7. Serve immediately, optionally with a chopped salad for rolling up.

Stuffed Tomatoes

 10 servings   45 minutes

INGREDIENTS

- 9 ripe medium-sized tomatoes
- 1 egg
- 3 large tablespoons breadcrumbs
- 1 clove garlic (optional)
- 9 black olives
- 100 - 120 g feta cheese
- Olive oil
- Basil leaves for garnish

DIRECTIONS

1. Rinse the tomatoes, remove their tops, and hollow them out with a small spoon. Don't discard the pulp and juice - you can use them for sauce or other dishes. Place the hollowed-out tomatoes upside down on a plate to drain.
2. Beat the egg and mix it with breadcrumbs, finely chopped garlic (if using), chopped black olives, and diced feta cheese. If the mixture is too dry, add a tablespoon or two of the drained tomato juice. No need to add salt as feta cheese is already salty.
3. Stuff the drained tomatoes with the prepared mixture, drizzle with olive oil, and place them on a greased baking tray.
4. Bake in a preheated oven at 200°C (400°F) for 20 minutes.
5. Garnish the baked tomatoes with fresh basil leaves and serve hot.

Eggplant Dolma

 10 servings   2 hrs

INGREDIENTS

For the eggplants:

- 6-8 small to medium eggplants
- Salt for sprinkling

For the filling:

- 500g ground lamb (or beef)
- 1 medium onion, finely chopped
- 1/2 cup rice, rinsed
- 1/4 cup fresh herbs (mix of parsley, cilantro, and dill), chopped
- 1 tsp salt
- 1/2 tsp black pepper
- 1/2 tsp ground cumin

For the sauce:

- 2 tbsp tomato paste
- 2 cups water
- 2 tbsp butter
- Salt to taste

- This dish is often served as a main course and is particularly popular during summer when eggplants are in season.

DIRECTIONS

1. Prepare the eggplants:
   - Cut the stems off the eggplants and peel strips of skin lengthwise, creating a striped pattern.
   - Cut each eggplant in half lengthwise, then scoop out the flesh, leaving a thin shell.
   - Sprinkle salt on the eggplant halves and let sit for 30 minutes to remove bitterness.
2. Make the filling:
   - Mix ground lamb, chopped onion, rice, herbs, salt, pepper, and cumin in a bowl.
3. Stuff the eggplants:
   - Rinse and pat dry the eggplant halves.
   - Fill each eggplant half with the meat mixture, but don't overstuff.
4. Prepare for cooking:
   - Arrange the stuffed eggplants in a large, deep pan.
5. Make the sauce:
   - Mix tomato paste with water.
   - Pour the mixture over the stuffed eggplants.
   - Add butter and additional salt if needed.
6. Cook the dolma:
   - Bring to a boil, then reduce heat to low.
   - Cover and simmer for about 40-45 minutes, or until the eggplants are tender and the filling is cooked through.
7. Serve:
   - Carefully transfer the eggplant dolma to a serving plate.
   - Spoon some of the cooking liquid over the top.
   - Serve hot, optionally with a dollop of yogurt on the side.

Plov with Pumpkin

 10 servings   2 hrs

INGREDIENTS

- 2 cups long-grain rice (preferably Basmati)
- 500g pumpkin, peeled and cut into 1-inch cubes
- 2 onions, finely chopped
- 1/2 cup vegetable oil or clarified butter (ghee)
- 1/2 cup dried fruits (mix of raisins, dried apricots, and/or prunes)
- 1/4 cup chopped chestnuts (optional)
- 2 tsp salt
- 1 tsp ground cinnamon
- 1/2 tsp ground cardamom
- 1/4 tsp saffron threads, soaked in 2 tbsp hot water
- 4 cups hot water or broth

DIRECTIONS

Prepare the rice:
- Rinse the rice thoroughly until the water runs clear.
- Soak the rice in warm, salted water for 30 minutes, then drain.

Cook the pumpkin and onions:
- In a large, heavy-bottomed pot, heat the oil over medium heat.
- Add the chopped onions and cook until golden, about 10 minutes.
- Add the pumpkin cubes and cook for another 5-7 minutes, stirring occasionally.

Add spices and dried fruits:
- Stir in the cinnamon, cardamom, and dried fruits.
- Cook for 2-3 minutes to allow the flavors to meld.

Cook the rice:
- Add the drained rice to the pot, stirring gently to coat with oil and spices.
- Pour in the hot water or broth and add salt. Stir once.
- Bring to a boil, then reduce heat to low.
- Cover and simmer for about 20 minutes, or until the rice is tender and liquid is absorbed.

Add saffron and steam:
- Drizzle the saffron water over the rice.
- Cover the pot with a clean kitchen towel, then replace the lid.
- Let steam on very low heat for another 10 minutes.

Sini Manti (Armenian Baked Dumplings)

 2 servings   30 min

INGREDIENTS

For the dough:

- 3 cups all-purpose flour
- 1 tsp salt
- 2 eggs
- 1/2 cup water

For the filling:

- 1 lb ground lamb (or beef)
- 1 small onion, finely minced
- 2 cloves garlic, minced
- 1/4 cup chopped parsley
- 1 tsp salt
- 1/2 tsp black pepper

For the broth:

- 4 cups lamb or beef broth
- 1 cup tomato sauce
- Salt to taste

For serving:

- 2 cups plain yogurt mixed with 2 minced garlic cloves
- Aleppo pepper
- Sumac

DIRECTIONS

1. Make the dough: Mix flour and salt. Add eggs and water, knead until smooth. Rest for 30 minutes.
2. Prepare filling: Combine all filling ingredients.
3. Roll out dough very thin. Cut into 2-inch squares.
4. Place a small amount of filling in the center of each square. Pinch two opposite corners together to form a canoe shape.
5. Arrange manti closely in a greased baking dish.
6. Bake at 375°F for 25-30 minutes until golden and crisp.
7. Meanwhile, simmer broth and tomato sauce together.
8. Pour hot broth over baked manti. Let stand for 5-10 minutes.
9. Serve topped with garlicky yogurt, Aleppo pepper, and sumac.

Shepherd's Salad

 4 servings   20 minutes

INGREDIENTS

- 3 medium tomatoes, diced
- 2 cucumbers, diced
- 1 green bell pepper, diced
- 1 small red onion, finely chopped
- 1/2 cup fresh parsley, finely chopped
- 2 tablespoons extra virgin olive oil
- Juice of 1 lemon
- Salt and freshly ground black pepper to taste
- Optional: 1/2 cup crumbled feta cheese
- Optional: chopped fresh mint

- The salad is best when served immediately, but can be refrigerated for a short time.
- While traditionally made without cheese, some variations include crumbled feta.
- This salad is especially popular during summer when vegetables are at their peak.

DIRECTIONS

Instructions:

1. Prepare the vegetables:
   - Wash all vegetables thoroughly.
   - Dice tomatoes, cucumbers, and green bell pepper into small, uniform pieces.
   - Finely chop the red onion and parsley.
2. Combine ingredients:
   - In a large bowl, mix together the diced tomatoes, cucumbers, green bell pepper, and chopped onion.
   - Add the chopped parsley to the vegetable mixture.
3. Dress the salad:
   - Drizzle the olive oil over the vegetables.
   - Squeeze the lemon juice over the salad.
   - Season with salt and freshly ground black pepper to taste.
4. Mix and marinate:
   - Gently toss all ingredients together until well combined.
   - Let the salad sit for about 10-15 minutes to allow the flavors to meld.
5. Serve:
   - Give the salad a final gentle toss before serving.
   - If using, sprinkle crumbled feta cheese on top.
   - Serve with crusty bread on the side.

Armenian Rice Pilaf

 6 servings 35 minutes

INGREDIENTS

- 2 cups long-grain white rice
- 1/4 cup vermicelli or thin egg noodles, broken into small pieces
- 4 tablespoons unsalted butter
- 4 cups chicken stock
- 1 teaspoon salt (adjust based on saltiness of stock)
- 1/4 teaspoon black pepper

DIRECTIONS

1. Rinse the rice in cold water until the water runs clear. Drain well.
2. In a medium saucepan, melt the butter over medium heat.
3. Add the broken vermicelli or noodles to the butter. Stir constantly until the pasta turns golden brown, about 2-3 minutes.
4. Add the drained rice to the pan. Stir to coat the rice with butter and continue cooking for another 2-3 minutes until the rice becomes slightly translucent.
5. Carefully pour in the chicken stock (it may splatter). Add salt and pepper.
6. Bring the mixture to a boil, then reduce heat to low. Cover the pan tightly with a lid.
7. Simmer for about 18-20 minutes, or until the liquid is absorbed and the rice is tender.
8. Remove from heat and let stand, covered, for 5-10 minutes.
9. Fluff the pilaf with a fork before serving.

Cabbage salad

 2 servings   10 minutes

INGREDIENTS

- 1 small cabbage (about 1 lb), thinly sliced
- 2 medium carrots, grated
- Salt, to taste
- 1 tablespoon sugar
- 2 tablespoons vinegar
- 1 teaspoon mustard
- 1/4 cup sour cream or plain yogurt

DIRECTIONS

1. **Prepare the Vegetables:**
   - Thinly slice the cabbage and grate the carrots. Place them in a large mixing bowl.
2. **Make the Dressing:**
   - In a small bowl, whisk together the sugar, vinegar, mustard, and sour cream (or yogurt) until well combined.
3. **Combine Ingredients:**
   - Pour the dressing over the cabbage and carrots in the mixing bowl.
4. **Season and Toss:**
   - Add salt to taste and toss the salad until the vegetables are evenly coated with the dressing.
5. **Chill and Serve:**
   - Refrigerate the salad for at least 30 minutes before serving to allow the flavors to meld together.

Ganach Lupia (Tomato-Braised Green Beans)

 6 servings 2 hrs

INGREDIENTS

- 2 lbs fresh green beans, ends trimmed
- 1 large onion, finely chopped (about 2 cups)
- 4 cloves garlic, minced
- 1/4 cup olive oil
- 1 (28 oz) can crushed tomatoes
- 1 cup water
- 1 lb beef stew meat, cut into 1-inch cubes (optional)
- 2 tsp salt
- 1/2 tsp black pepper
- 1/4 tsp red pepper flakes (optional)

Note: For a vegetarian version, simply omit the beef and use vegetable broth instead of water for more flavor.

DIRECTIONS

1. If using beef, season it with salt and pepper. In a large pot, heat 2 tablespoons of olive oil over medium-high heat. Brown the beef on all sides, about 5-7 minutes. Remove and set aside.
2. In the same pot, heat the remaining olive oil. Add onions and cook until softened, about 5 minutes.
3. Add garlic and cook for another minute until fragrant.
4. Return the beef to the pot (if using). Add green beans, crushed tomatoes, water, salt, pepper, and red pepper flakes if using.
5. Bring to a boil, then reduce heat to low. Cover and simmer for 2-3 hours, stirring occasionally, until the beans are very tender and the sauce has thickened.
6. Taste and adjust seasoning if necessary.
7. Serve hot as a main dish with rice or bread.

Havabour Soup (Chicken and Wheat Soup)

🍴 6 servings   🕐 40 min

INGREDIENTS

- 1 whole chicken (about 3-4 lbs), cut into pieces
- 1 cup wheat berries (or pearled barley)
- 1 large onion, finely chopped
- 2 carrots, diced
- 2 celery stalks, diced
- 2 cloves garlic, minced
- 2 tablespoons butter
- 8 cups water
- 2 bay leaves
- 1 teaspoon dried thyme
- Salt and pepper to taste
- 1/4 cup fresh parsley, chopped
- Lemon wedges for serving

It's often served as a main course and is considered a healing soup in Armenian culture, often prepared for those recovering from illness.

DIRECTIONS

1. Rinse the wheat berries and soak them in cold water for at least 4 hours or overnight.
2. In a large pot, melt the butter over medium heat. Add the onion, carrots, and celery. Sauté until the vegetables are softened, about 5 minutes.
3. Add the minced garlic and cook for another minute.
4. Add the chicken pieces to the pot and cook for a few minutes until they start to brown slightly.
5. Pour in the water, add bay leaves and thyme. Bring to a boil, then reduce heat and simmer for about 1 hour, or until the chicken is cooked through.
6. Remove the chicken from the pot. When cool enough to handle, remove the meat from the bones and shred it. Discard the skin and bones.
7. Drain the soaked wheat berries and add them to the pot. Simmer for another 30-40 minutes, or until the wheat is tender.
8. Return the shredded chicken to the pot. Season with salt and pepper to taste.
9. Simmer for an additional 10 minutes to reheat the chicken and meld the flavors.
10. Remove the bay leaves before serving.
11. Serve hot, garnished with fresh parsley and lemon wedges on the side.

Harissa (Wheat and Meat Porridge)

 6 servings   2 hrs

INGREDIENTS

- 2 cups korkot (shelled wheat berries)
- 1 lb boneless chicken or lamb, cut into large chunks
- 8 cups water or low-sodium chicken broth
- 1 tsp salt (adjust if using salted broth)
- 1/4 tsp black pepper

For the topping:
- 1/4 cup unsalted butter
- 2 tsp Aleppo pepper

DIRECTIONS

1. Rinse the wheat berries thoroughly.
2. In a large, heavy-bottomed pot, combine wheat berries, meat, water or broth, salt, and pepper.
3. Bring to a boil, then reduce heat to low. Simmer, partially covered, for about 3 hours, stirring occasionally.
4. As the mixture thickens, stir more frequently to prevent sticking. Add more hot water if needed.
5. When the meat is falling apart and the wheat is very soft, remove from heat.
6. Use a wooden spoon or immersion blender to mash the mixture into a uniform consistency.
7. Return to low heat and cook, stirring constantly, for another 15-20 minutes until very thick.
8. For the topping: Melt butter in a small pan. Add Aleppo pepper and cook until the butter is lightly browned and fragrant.
9. Serve the harissa hot, drizzled with the Aleppo pepper butter.

Eetch (Bulgur and Tomato Dish)

  6 servings   40 min

INGREDIENTS

- 1 cup fine bulgur wheat
- 1 cup hot water
- 2 medium tomatoes, finely diced (about 1 1/2 cups)
- 1 small onion, finely minced (about 1/2 cup)
- 1/4 cup olive oil
- 2 tablespoons tomato paste
- 1/2 cup finely chopped parsley
- 1/4 cup finely chopped mint
- 2 tablespoons lemon juice
- 1 teaspoon Aleppo pepper (or paprika)
- Salt to taste
- Black pepper to taste

For serving:
- Lettuce leaves or lavash bread

DIRECTIONS

1. Place bulgur in a large bowl and pour hot water over it. Cover and let stand for 30 minutes until the bulgur is tender and water is absorbed.
2. In a separate bowl, mix diced tomatoes, minced onion, olive oil, and tomato paste.
3. Add the tomato mixture to the softened bulgur and mix well.
4. Stir in chopped parsley, mint, lemon juice, Aleppo pepper, salt, and black pepper.
5. Taste and adjust seasoning if needed.
6. Cover and refrigerate for at least an hour to allow flavors to meld.
7. Before serving, let it come to room temperature and adjust seasoning again if necessary.
8. Serve as is, or with lettuce leaves or lavash bread for wrapping.

Eetch can be served as part of a mezze spread or as a light main dish. It's a versatile dish that's particularly refreshing in summer, but can be enjoyed year-round. The combination of bulgur, tomatoes, and fresh herbs creates a flavorful and satisfying dish that's both nutritious and easy to prepare. Unlike tabbouleh, eetch has a moister, more cohesive texture, making it ideal for stuffing into lettuce leaves or wrapping in lavash.

Tourshi (Armenian Pickled Vegetables)

 6 servings   🕐 90 minutes

INGREDIENTS

- 2 lbs mixed crisp vegetables (such as carrots, cauliflower, cabbage, and turnips), cut into bite-sized pieces
- 4 cups water
- 2 cups white vinegar
- 2 tablespoons kosher salt
- 1 tablespoon sugar
- 2 teaspoons mustard seeds
- 2 teaspoons coriander seeds
- 1 teaspoon black peppercorns
- 1 teaspoon allspice berries
- 4 cloves garlic, peeled and lightly crushed
- 2 bay leaves

Note: This recipe uses a vinegar-based brine rather than fermentation. The pickles will keep for several months when properly stored. Always use clean utensils when removing pickles from the jar to prevent contamination.

DIRECTIONS

1. Wash and prepare your chosen vegetables, cutting them into bite-sized pieces.
2. In a large pot, combine water, vinegar, salt, and sugar. Bring to a boil, stirring to dissolve the salt and sugar.
3. Add mustard seeds, coriander seeds, peppercorns, allspice berries, garlic cloves, and bay leaves to the brine. Simmer for 5 minutes.
4. Pack the prepared vegetables tightly into clean, sterilized jars.
5. Carefully pour the hot brine over the vegetables, making sure to distribute the spices evenly among the jars. Ensure the vegetables are completely covered by the brine.
6. Let the jars cool to room temperature, then seal them tightly with lids.
7. Store the jars in a cool, dark place for at least 2-3 weeks before consuming to allow the flavors to develop.
8. Once opened, store in the refrigerator.

Serving suggestions:
1. Serve as part of a mezze spread
2. Use as a side dish for main courses
3. Enjoy as a tangy snack or appetizer

Canned Tomatoes

🍴 6 servings   🕐 90 minutes

INGREDIENTS

- About 600 g / 1.2 lb of tomatoes
- 1 tablespoon of lemon juice

DIRECTIONS

1. Cut a small "X" on the bottom of each tomato and score the top with a small cross.
2. Place the tomatoes in a bowl and cover them with boiling water. Let them sit for 1 minute, then transfer them to cold water. After a few minutes, peel the skin off the tomatoes.
3. Cut the peeled tomatoes in half and place them in sterilized jars. Pack the tomatoes tightly into the jars, pressing down with a spoon to release any air bubbles and ensure they are filled with tomato juice.
4. Leave about 1.5 cm of space from the top of the jar, then add lemon juice and cover with a lid, but do not tighten it completely.
5. The next step is pasteurization. Place the jars in a large pot lined with a towel or rack. Fill the pot with water up to the neck of the jars. Bring the pot to a boil, then let the jars boil for 1 hour.
6. Carefully remove the jars from the water, tighten the lids completely, invert the jars with the lids down, and let them cool.

Choreg (Armenian Easter Bread)

🍴 4 servings 🕐 2 hrs

INGREDIENTS

- 4 1/2 cups all-purpose flour
- 1/2 cup granulated sugar
- 2 1/4 tsp active dry yeast
- 1 tsp salt
- 1 tsp ground mahlab
- 1/2 tsp ground nigella seeds
- 1 cup whole milk, warmed
- 2 large eggs, room temperature
- 1/2 cup (1 stick) unsalted butter, melted and cooled
- 1 tsp vanilla extract
- 1 egg beaten with 1 tbsp water (for egg wash)
- Sesame seeds for topping (optional)

DIRECTIONS

1. In a large bowl, whisk together flour, sugar, yeast, salt, mahlab, and nigella seeds.
2. In another bowl, combine warm milk, eggs, melted butter, and vanilla extract.
3. Pour the wet ingredients into the dry ingredients. Mix until a soft dough forms.
4. Knead the dough on a floured surface for about 10 minutes until smooth and elastic.
5. Place the dough in a greased bowl, cover, and let rise in a warm place for about 2 hours or until doubled in size.
6. Punch down the dough and divide it into 12 equal pieces for rolls or 3 pieces for a braid.
7. Shape as desired (rounds, knots, or braid).
8. Place shaped dough on a baking sheet lined with parchment paper. Cover and let rise for another 1 hour.
9. Preheat oven to 350°F (175°C).
10. Brush the loaves with egg wash and sprinkle with sesame seeds if desired.
11. Bake for 25-30 minutes for rolls or 35-40 minutes for a braid, until golden brown.
12. Cool on a wire rack before serving.

Apricot Preserves

🍴 4 servings   🕐 60 minutes

INGREDIENTS

- 2 lbs fresh apricots, pitted and chopped
- 2 cups granulated sugar
- Juice of 1 lemon
- 1 teaspoon cardamom powder
- 1/2 teaspoon almond extract (optional)

DIRECTIONS

1. Prepare Apricots (20 minutes):
- Wash, pit, and chop the fresh apricots.
2. Cook Apricots (30 minutes):
- In a large pot, combine chopped apricots, granulated sugar, and lemon juice. Cook over medium heat, stirring frequently, until the apricots break down and the mixture thickens.
3. Add Cardamom (10 minutes):
- Stir in cardamom powder, allowing it to infuse its aromatic flavor into the preserves. Continue cooking for an additional 10 minutes.
4. Check Consistency (10 minutes):
- To test the consistency, place a small amount of the preserves on a cold plate. If it wrinkles and holds its shape, it's ready.
5. Add Almond Extract (5 minutes):
- If desired, stir in almond extract for an extra layer of flavor. Remove the pot from heat.
6. Cool (15 minutes):
- Allow to cool slightly.
7. Jar (10 minutes):
- Spoon the preserves into sterilized jars, leaving a little space at the top. Seal the jars tightly.
8. Cool Completely (20 minutes):
- Let the jars cool completely before storing them in the refrigerator.
9. Serve (5 minutes):
- Serve these delightful Preserves on toast, as a topping for desserts, or as a sweet addition to your favorite dishes.

Tarragon Lemonade

 10 servings   15 min

INGREDIENTS

- 1 cup fresh lemon juice (about 4-6 lemons)
- 1 cup granulated sugar (adjust to taste)
- 6 cups cold water
- 1/4 cup fresh tarragon leaves, chopped
- Ice cubes
- Lemon slices and tarragon sprigs for garnish (optional)

DIRECTIONS

1. **Make Simple Syrup:**
   - In a small saucepan, combine 1 cup of water with the granulated sugar. Heat over medium heat, stirring occasionally until the sugar completely dissolves. This creates a simple syrup. Remove from heat and let it cool.

2. **Infuse Tarragon:**
   - Add the chopped tarragon leaves to the simple syrup while it's still warm. Let it steep for about 15-20 minutes. This allows the tarragon flavor to infuse into the syrup. Strain the syrup to remove the tarragon leaves.

3. **Prepare Lemon Juice:**
   - Squeeze enough lemons to obtain 1 cup of fresh lemon juice.

4. **Combine Lemon Juice and Syrup:**
   - In a large pitcher, combine the fresh lemon juice with the tarragon-infused simple syrup.

5. **Add Cold Water:**
   - Pour 6 cups of cold water into the pitcher. Stir well to combine.

6. **Chill:**
   - Place the pitcher in the refrigerator to chill the lemonade.

7. **Serve:**
   - Once the lemonade is chilled, serve it over ice cubes in glasses.

8. **Garnish (Optional):**
   - Garnish each glass with a slice of lemon and a sprig of tarragon for a decorative touch.

9. **Enjoy:**
   - Stir the lemonade before serving to make sure the flavors are well distributed. Enjoy the unique and refreshing taste of Tarragon Lemonade!

Baked apple

 4 servings   20 min

INGREDIENTS

- 6 medium apples
- 1/2 cup raisins
- 4 tbsp apricot jam
- 4 tbsp lemon juice (from 1 medium lemon)
- 1 tsp cinnamon
- 1 tbsp sugar
- 1/2 cup walnuts, chopped
- 1 and 1/2 tbsp butter (20 g), cut into small pieces

DIRECTIONS

1. **Preheat Oven and Prepare Baking Dish:**
   - Preheat your oven to 375°F (190°C).
   - Lightly butter a baking dish large enough to fit all the apples.

2. **Prepare the Apples:**
   - Core the apples, making sure to leave the bottoms intact to create a well for the stuffing.
   - Peel the top third of each apple to prevent the skin from splitting during baking. Place the apples in the prepared dish.

3. **Make the Filling:**
   - In a bowl, mix together the raisins, chopped walnuts, apricot jam, cinnamon, and lemon juice.
   - Stuff each apple with the raisin and walnut mixture, pressing it in firmly.

4. **Top and Season:**
   - Sprinkle the top of each stuffed apple with sugar.
   - Dot each apple with pieces of butter.

5. **Bake the Apples:**
   - Pour a small amount of water into the bottom of the baking dish to prevent the apples from sticking (about 1/4 inch deep).
   - Bake in the preheated oven for about 30-40 minutes, or until the apples are tender but not collapsing.

6. **Serving:**
   - Serve the baked apples warm, ideally with a scoop of vanilla ice cream or a drizzle of cream for extra indulgence.

"Gift" Cake (Tort "Nver")

🍴 8 servings   🕐 1 hr

INGREDIENTS

For the Cake:
- 4 large eggs, separated
- 1 cup (120g) all-purpose flour
- 1/2 cup (120g) granulated sugar
- 1/4 teaspoon vanilla extract
- 1 cup (120g) peanuts

For the Syrup:
- 1/2 cup water
- 1/2 cup (100g) granulated sugar

For the Cream:
- 3/4 cup whole milk
- 3/4 cup (150g) granulated sugar
- 3 large eggs
- 1 cup (225g) unsalted butter, softened
- 1 teaspoon vanilla extract

Serving suggestion: This rich, nutty cake is perfect for special occasions. The combination of light sponge, creamy filling, and crunchy peanuts creates a delightful texture contrast.

DIRECTIONS

1. Preheat oven to 350°F (180°C). Grease and line a 9-inch round cake pan with parchment paper.
2. Beat egg whites with half the sugar until stiff peaks form. In another bowl, beat yolks with remaining sugar until pale and creamy.
3. Gently fold egg white mixture into yolk mixture. Sift in flour and fold carefully.
4. Pour batter into prepared pan. Bake for 35 minutes or until a toothpick comes out clean.
5. Cool in pan for 10 minutes, then remove and split into two layers.
6. For syrup: Dissolve sugar in water over medium heat. Cool.
7. Toast peanuts in a dry pan or in the oven at 400°F (200°C) for 5-7 minutes. Chop coarsely when cool.
8. For cream: Whisk milk, sugar, and eggs in a saucepan over medium heat until thickened. Cool completely. Beat in softened butter and vanilla until fluffy.
9. Brush cake layers with syrup. Spread cream between layers and over the entire cake.
10. Decorate with chopped peanuts.

Lake Sevan Region

Nut Stuffed Trout

🍴 12 servings 🕐 1 hour

INGREDIENTS

For the main dish:
- 1 large trout
- Salt and pepper to taste

For the stuffing:
- 2 cups walnuts, finely chopped
- 2 large onions, finely chopped
- 1/2 cup raisins
- 1/4 cup dried apricots pitted and chopped (or substitute with dried sour plums)
- 2 tbsp narsharab (pomegranate molasses)
- 1 tbsp sumac
- Salt and pepper to taste

DIRECTIONS

Prepare the main ingredient:
- Clean, scale, and remove gills. Make a pocket in the belly for stuffing.

Make the stuffing:
- In a large bowl, mix chopped walnuts, onions, raisins, apricots, narsharab, and sumac.
- Season with salt and pepper. The mixture should be moist but not wet.

Stuff and prepare for cooking:
- For chicken: Stuff the mixture under the skin and inside the cavity.
- For fish: Stuff the mixture into the belly pocket.
- Season the outside with salt and pepper.

Cook:
- Preheat oven to 180°C (350°F).
- Place the stuffed chicken or fish in a baking dish.
- For fish: Bake for about 40-50 minutes, or until the fish flakes easily.

Serve:
- Let rest for 10 minutes before serving.

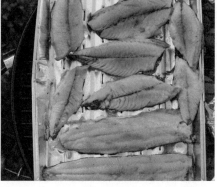

Baked Fish in Lavash (Armenian Fish Rolls)

 12 servings   1 hour

INGREDIENTS

- 1 whole trout (about 1.5 lbs), cleaned and filleted
- 2 large sheets of lavash bread
- 1 medium onion, thinly sliced
- 1/2 lemon, thinly sliced
- 1 bunch fresh dill, chopped
- 6 tablespoons (80g) unsalted butter, softened
- 1 teaspoon salt
- 1/4 teaspoon ground black pepper
- 1 teaspoon mixed herbs (optional)

Serve hot, garnished with fresh tarragon sprigs and pomegranate seeds if desired. These fish rolls pair well with rice, potatoes, or a fresh vegetable salad.

Note: Lavash is a thin flatbread common in Armenian cuisine. If unavailable, you can substitute with thin flour tortillas or phyllo dough.

DIRECTIONS

1. Preheat oven to 325°F (160°C).
2. Cut the fish into 4 equal portions. Season with salt and pepper.
3. Cut each lavash sheet in half to make 4 pieces total.
4. In a small bowl, mix sliced onion, lemon, and chopped dill.
5. On each piece of lavash, place some of the onion-lemon-dill mixture.
6. Place a portion of fish on top of the mixture on each lavash piece.
7. Top the fish with more of the onion-lemon-dill mixture and about 1 tablespoon of butter.
8. Roll up each lavash piece to enclose the fish, tucking in the sides as you roll.
9. Brush the outside of each roll with remaining softened butter.
10. Place the rolls in a buttered baking dish.
11. Bake for 30 minutes, or until the fish is cooked through and the lavash is golden brown.

Fish Khashlama

 12 servings 1 hour

INGREDIENTS

- 2 lbs (900g) white fish fillets (trout or cod), cut into large chunks
- 2 large onions, sliced
- 3 medium tomatoes, sliced
- 2 bell peppers, sliced
- 3 medium potatoes, peeled and sliced
- 2 carrots, sliced
- 4 cloves garlic, minced
- Juice of 1 lemon
- 1/4 cup (60ml) olive oil
- 1/4 cup fresh parsley, chopped
- 2 tbsp fresh dill, chopped
- 2 tbsp fresh cilantro, chopped
- 1 tsp salt
- 1/2 tsp black pepper
- 2 bay leaves
- 1/2 cup (120ml) water

DIRECTIONS

1. In a large, deep pot or casserole dish, layer ingredients in this order:
   - 1/3 of the onions
   - 1/2 of the potatoes
   - 1/2 of the carrots
   - 1/2 of the bell peppers
   - 1/3 of the onions
2. All of the fish chunks
3. Remaining vegetables
4. Sprinkle each layer with some of the salt, pepper, and herbs.
5. Add minced garlic on top.
6. Drizzle with olive oil and lemon juice.
7. Add bay leaves.
8. Pour in 1/2 cup of water.
9. Cover tightly and cook on low heat for 45-50 minutes.
10. Let rest for 5 minutes before serving.

Armenian Stuffed Mussels

 12 servings   1 hour

INGREDIENTS

- 2 lbs fresh mussels, cleaned and debearded
- 1 cup short-grain rice
- 1 large onion, finely chopped
- 1/4 cup pine nuts
- 1/4 cup currants
- 1/4 cup chopped fresh parsley
- 2 tbsp chopped fresh dill
- 2 tbsp olive oil
- 1 tsp ground cinnamon
- 1/2 tsp allspice
- 1/4 tsp black pepper
- Salt to taste
- Lemon wedges for serving

DIRECTIONS

1. Rinse the rice and soak it in warm water for 30 minutes. Drain.
2. In a pan, heat olive oil and sauté the onion until translucent.
3. Add pine nuts and currants, cook for 2-3 minutes.
4. Add the drained rice, spices, salt, and 1 cup of water. Simmer covered until rice is partially cooked (about 10 minutes).
5. Remove from heat, stir in parsley and dill. Let cool.
6. Clean the mussels thoroughly. Steam them just until they open slightly.
7. Carefully pry open each mussel, keeping the halves attached.
8. Stuff each mussel with a spoonful of the rice mixture.
9. Arrange the stuffed mussels in a large pot, stacking them if necessary.
10. Add 1/2 cup of water to the pot. Cover and steam over low heat for about 15-20 minutes, until mussels are fully opened and filling is hot.
11. Serve warm or at room temperature with lemon wedges.

Oyster Plaki

 12 servings   15 min

INGREDIENTS

- 24 fresh oysters, shucked, with bottom shells reserved
- 1/4 cup olive oil
- 1 large onion, finely chopped
- 3 cloves garlic, minced
- 2 medium tomatoes, diced
- 1/4 cup chopped fresh parsley
- 2 tablespoons chopped fresh dill
- 1/4 cup dry white wine
- 2 tablespoons lemon juice
- 1/2 cup breadcrumbs
- Salt and freshly ground black pepper to taste
- Lemon wedges for serving

DIRECTIONS

1. Preheat the oven to 375°F (190°C).
2. In a large skillet, heat the olive oil over medium heat. Add the onion and garlic, and sauté until softened, about 5 minutes.
3. Add the diced tomatoes, parsley, and dill. Cook for another 5 minutes until the tomatoes start to break down.
4. Pour in the white wine and lemon juice. Simmer for 2-3 minutes to reduce slightly.
5. Season the mixture with salt and pepper to taste.
6. Arrange the oyster shells on a baking sheet. Place an oyster in each shell.
7. Spoon the tomato mixture over each oyster, dividing it evenly.
8. Sprinkle breadcrumbs over the top of each oyster.
9. Bake in the preheated oven for 10-12 minutes, or until the breadcrumbs are golden brown and the oysters are just cooked through.
10. Serve hot with lemon wedges on the side.

Grilled Mackerel

Summer staple

 4 servings   30 minutes

INGREDIENTS

- 4 fresh mackerel fillets
- 2 tablespoons olive oil
- 2 tablespoons lemon juice
- 2 cloves garlic, minced
- 1 teaspoon paprika
- 1 teaspoon dried oregano
- Salt and pepper, to taste
- Fresh parsley, chopped (for garnish)
- Lemon wedges, for serving

DIRECTIONS

1. Preheat the grill to medium-high heat.
2. In a small bowl, combine the olive oil, lemon juice, minced garlic, paprika, dried oregano, salt, and pepper. Mix well to create a marinade.
3. Place the mackerel fillets in a shallow dish or resealable plastic bag. Pour the marinade over the fish, making sure all the fillets are evenly coated. Let them marinate for about 15-30 minutes to allow the flavors to infuse into the fish.
4. Remove the mackerel fillets from the marinade and place them on the preheated grill, skin-side down. Grill for about 4-5 minutes per side, or until the fish is cooked through and has nice grill marks.
5. While grilling, you can baste the fish occasionally with the leftover marinade to enhance the flavors.
6. Once cooked, transfer the grilled mackerel fillets to a serving platter. Sprinkle them with freshly chopped parsley for added freshness and garnish.
7. Serve the Bulgarian Grilled Mackerel hot, accompanied by lemon wedges for squeezing over the fish. This flavorful and healthy dish is a staple in Bulgarian cuisine and is best enjoyed with a side of fresh salad or grilled vegetables.

Fish Kabob with Pomegranate Glaze

🍴 20 servings   🕐 100 minutes

INGREDIENTS

For the Fish Kabob:

- 1 lb white fish fillets (such as pike or catfish), cut into chunks
- 1 red onion, cut into chunks
- 1 bell pepper (any color), cut into chunks
- Cherry tomatoes
- Wooden skewers, soaked in water

For the Pomegranate Glaze:

- 1 cup pomegranate juice
- 2 tablespoons honey
- 1 tablespoon soy sauce
- 1 tablespoon olive oil
- 1 teaspoon ground cumin
- 1 teaspoon paprika
- Salt and pepper to taste
- Fresh parsley for garnish (optional)

DIRECTIONS

For the Pomegranate Glaze:

1. In a small saucepan, combine pomegranate juice, honey, soy sauce, olive oil, ground cumin, paprika, salt, and pepper. Bring to a simmer over medium heat.
2. Reduce the heat and let the glaze simmer for about 15 minutes, or until it thickens to a syrupy consistency. Stir occasionally.
3. Allow the glaze to cool. It will continue to thicken as it cools.

For the Fish Kabob:

1. Place fish chunks in a bowl and generously brush them with the pomegranate glaze. Allow the fish to marinate for at least 30 minutes, or refrigerate for a few hours for better flavor.
2. Preheat the grill or oven. Thread marinated fish chunks, red onion chunks, bell pepper chunks, and cherry tomatoes onto the soaked wooden skewers, alternating the ingredients.
3. Grill the fish skewers over medium-high heat for 4-5 minutes per side or until the fish is cooked through and has a nice char. Alternatively, you can bake them in a preheated oven at 400°F (200°C) for 8-10 minutes, turning halfway through.
4. During the last few minutes of cooking, brush the fish skewers with the pomegranate glaze for an extra layer of flavor.
5. Transfer the Fish Kabobs to a serving platter. Garnish with fresh parsley if desired. Serve with extra pomegranate glaze on the side.

Bozbash (Vegetable and Chicken Soup)

 20 servings   50 min

INGREDIENTS

- 1 lb (450g) chicken breast, cut into cubes
- 1 large onion, chopped
- 2 bell peppers, chopped
- 2 cups green beans, trimmed and cut into 1-inch pieces
- 2 large potatoes, peeled and cubed
- 1 can (15 oz) chickpeas, drained and rinsed
- 2 tbsp tomato paste
- 2 tbsp red pepper paste
- 8 cups chicken broth
- 2 tbsp olive oil
- 2 bay leaves
- Salt and black pepper to taste
- Fresh parsley for garnish

DIRECTIONS

1. Prepare the base:
   - In a large pot, heat olive oil over medium heat.
   - Add chopped onions and sauté until translucent, about 5 minutes.
2. Cook the chicken:
   - Add chicken cubes to the pot and cook until they start to brown, about 5-7 minutes.
3. Add vegetables:
   - Stir in bell peppers and green beans. Cook for another 5 minutes.
4. Incorporate remaining ingredients:
   - Add potatoes, chickpeas, tomato paste, and red pepper paste. Stir well to combine.
   - Pour in the chicken broth and add bay leaves.
   - Bring to a boil, then reduce heat and simmer for about 30 minutes, or until potatoes are tender.
5. Season and finish:
   - Add salt and black pepper to taste.
   - Simmer for an additional 5 minutes.
6. Serve:
   - Remove bay leaves before serving.
   - Ladle into bowls and garnish with fresh parsley.

Serve hot with crusty bread on the side. As they say in Armenia, "Bari akhorzhak" (Bon appétit)!

Grilled Vegetable Mezze

🍴 4 servings   🕐 40 minutes

INGREDIENTS

- 2 medium eggplants
- 3 large tomatoes
- 2 bell peppers (preferably different colors)
- 1 hot pepper (optional)
- 1 large onion
- 3 cloves of garlic, minced
- 1/4 cup olive oil
- Salt to taste
- Fresh herbs: 1/4 cup each of chopped cilantro, dill, and basil (or any combination)
- 1 tablespoon lemon juice (optional)

Serving suggestions:
- Serve as a side dish to grilled meats.
- Enjoy with fresh bread or lavash.
- Pair with Motal cheese

DIRECTIONS

Instructions:
1. Prepare the grill:
   - Heat your mangal or regular grill to medium-high heat.
2. Prepare the vegetables:
   - Wash all vegetables.
   - Cut eggplants and tomatoes in half lengthwise.
   - Leave bell peppers, hot pepper, and onion whole.
3. Grill the vegetables:
   - Place vegetables on the grill.
   - Grill for about 10-15 minutes, turning occasionally, until charred and softened.
   - The onion and peppers may take a bit longer than the eggplant and tomatoes.
4. Process the grilled vegetables:
   - Let the grilled vegetables cool slightly.
   - Peel the charred skin off the peppers and tomatoes.
   - Chop all vegetables into small pieces.
5. Assemble the salad:
   - In a large bowl, combine the chopped grilled vegetables.
   - Add minced garlic, olive oil, and salt.
   - Mix in the fresh herbs.
   - If using, add lemon juice for extra tanginess.
   - Toss everything together gently.
6. Serve:
   - Let the salad sit for about 15-30 minutes to allow flavors to meld.
   - Serve at room temperature or slightly chilled.

Walnut Stuffed Eggplant Rolls

 5servings 50 minutes

INGREDIENTS

For the Eggplant Rolls:

- 2 large eggplants, thinly sliced lengthwise
- 3 tablespoons olive oil
- Salt and pepper to taste

For the Walnut Filling:

- 1 cup walnuts, finely chopped
- 1/2 cup fresh breadcrumbs
- 1/4 cup fresh parsley, chopped
- 2 cloves garlic, minced
- 1 tablespoon lemon juice
- 2 tablespoons olive oil
- Salt and pepper to taste

For the Sauce:

- 1 cup plain Greek yogurt
- 1 tablespoon tahini
- 1 tablespoon lemon juice
- 1 tablespoon fresh mint, chopped
- Salt and pepper to taste

DIRECTIONS

For the Eggplant Rolls:

1. Preheat your oven to 375°F (190°C).
2. Slice the eggplants lengthwise into thin strips. Brush each strip with olive oil and season with salt and pepper.
3. Place the eggplant strips on a baking sheet and roast in the preheated oven for about 20 minutes or until they are tender and golden brown. Allow them to cool.

For the Walnut Filling:

1. In a bowl, mix together finely chopped walnuts, fresh breadcrumbs, chopped parsley, minced garlic, lemon juice, olive oil, salt, and pepper. Ensure a well-combined mixture.

Assemble the Rolls:

1. Place a spoonful of the walnut filling at one end of each eggplant strip. Roll the eggplant around the filling, creating a roll. Repeat for all slices.
2. Use toothpicks to secure the rolls and prevent them from unraveling.
3. Place the stuffed eggplant rolls in a baking dish and bake for an additional 15 minutes, allowing the flavors to meld.

For the Sauce:

1. In a bowl, mix together Greek yogurt, tahini, lemon juice, chopped fresh mint, salt, and pepper. This will be your creamy and flavorful sauce.

Salad with Pomegranate Dressing

 10 servings   30 minutes

INGREDIENTS

Salad:

- 4 cups mixed salad greens (lettuce, spinach, arugula)
- 1 cucumber, thinly sliced
- 1 cup cherry tomatoes, halved
- 1 red onion, thinly sliced
- 1 cup radishes, thinly sliced
- 1/2 cup fresh herbs (dill, mint, or parsley), chopped

Pomegranate Dressing:

- 1/4 cup pomegranate juice
- 2 tablespoons olive oil
- 1 tablespoon red wine vinegar
- 1 teaspoon honey
- Salt and pepper to taste

Garnish:

- 1/2 cup pomegranate arils
- 1/4 cup crumbled feta cheese (optional)

DIRECTIONS

1. Prepare Salad Greens (5 minutes):
- Wash and dry the mixed salad greens. Place them in a large salad bowl.
2. Add Vegetables (5 minutes):
- Add thinly sliced cucumber, halved cherry tomatoes, sliced red onion, and sliced radishes to the salad bowl.
3. Toss with Herbs (2 minutes):
- Toss the salad ingredients together with fresh herbs, such as dill, mint, or parsley.
4. Prepare Pomegranate Dressing (5 minutes):
- In a small bowl, whisk together pomegranate juice, olive oil, red wine vinegar, honey, salt, and pepper until well combined.
5. Drizzle Dressing (2 minutes):
- Drizzle the pomegranate dressing over the salad and toss gently to coat the ingredients evenly.
6. Garnish (2 minutes):
- Sprinkle pomegranate arils and crumbled feta cheese (if using) over the salad as a colorful and flavorful garnish.
7. Serve (2 minutes):
- Serve the refreshing Salad immediately, showcasing the vibrant colors and enticing flavors.
8. Enjoy (2 minutes):
- Enjoy the crispness of the greens, the sweetness of pomegranate, and the zesty dressing in this delightful Salad, a perfect accompaniment to any meal.

Jajic (Yogurt and Cucumber Dip)

 4 servings 25 min

INGREDIENTS

- 2 cups plain yogurt (preferably thick, strained yogurt or Greek yogurt)
- 1 large cucumber, peeled and finely diced
- 2-3 cloves of garlic, minced
- 2 tablespoons fresh dill, finely chopped
- 2 tablespoons fresh mint, finely chopped
- 1 tablespoon extra virgin olive oil
- 1 teaspoon salt (or to taste)
- 1/4 teaspoon black pepper
- Optional:
- 1 tablespoon lemon juice
- A pinch of sumac for garnish

DIRECTIONS

1. If your yogurt isn't thick enough, strain it through a cheesecloth for a couple of hours to remove excess liquid.
2. Peel and finely dice the cucumber. Place the diced cucumber in a colander, sprinkle with a little salt, and let it sit for about 30 minutes to draw out excess water.
3. Pat the cucumber dry with paper towels to remove as much moisture as possible.
4. In a medium bowl, combine the yogurt, drained cucumber, minced garlic, chopped dill, and mint.
5. Add olive oil, salt, and pepper. Mix well.
6. If using, add lemon juice and stir to combine.
7. Cover and refrigerate for at least an hour to allow flavors to meld.
8. Before serving, taste and adjust seasoning if needed.
9. Serve chilled, optionally garnished with a sprinkle of sumac and a drizzle of olive oil.
10. Jajic is typically served as a dip with pita bread or lavash, or as a side dish with grilled meats. It's also excellent as a condiment for kebabs or falafel. The cool, creamy texture and fresh flavors make it a perfect accompaniment to spicy dishes or as a refreshing snack on hot days.

In Armenian cuisine, Jajic might be slightly thicker than its Greek counterpart tzatziki, and the use of dill is more common. The combination of cool yogurt, crisp cucumber, and aromatic herbs makes this a beloved dish in Armenian households and beyond.

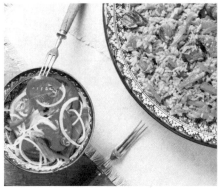

Achichuk Salad

🍴 4 servings   🕐 30 minutes

INGREDIENTS

For the Salad:

- 2 large tomatoes, diced
- 1 cucumber, diced
- 1 red onion, thinly sliced
- 1 green bell pepper, diced
- 1 red chili pepper, finely chopped (adjust to taste)
- 1/2 cup fresh parsley, chopped

For the Dressing:

- 3 tablespoons olive oil
- 2 tablespoons red wine vinegar
- 1 clove garlic, minced
- 1 teaspoon ground sumac
- Salt and pepper to taste

DIRECTIONS

1. **Prepare Vegetables (10 minutes):**
   - Dice the tomatoes and cucumber. Thinly slice the red onion. Dice the green bell pepper. Finely chop the red chili pepper (adjust the amount based on your spice preference). Chop fresh parsley.
2. **Combine Salad Ingredients (2 minutes):**
   - In a large bowl, combine the diced tomatoes, diced cucumber, thinly sliced red onion, diced green bell pepper, chopped red chili pepper, and fresh parsley. Toss gently to mix the ingredients.
3. **Prepare Dressing (3 minutes):**
   - In a small bowl, whisk together olive oil, red wine vinegar, minced garlic, ground sumac, salt, and pepper. Ensure a well-emulsified dressing.
4. **Drizzle Dressing (2 minutes):**
   - Drizzle the dressing over the salad. Toss the salad again to coat the vegetables evenly with the flavorful dressing.
5. **Adjust Seasoning (1 minute):**
   - Taste the salad and adjust the seasoning with salt and pepper if needed.
6. **Serve (2 minutes):**
   - Transfer the Achichuk Salad to a serving dish or individual plates.

Sumakh Sorbet

🍴 4 servings   🕐 20 min

INGREDIENTS

- 100g sumac
- 500g granulated sugar
- 1.5 liters water

Sumac grows wild in Azerbaijan and Armenia and is widely used in the cuisine.

DIRECTIONS

1. Prepare the syrup:
   - In a saucepan, combine the sugar and water.
   - Heat the mixture, stirring until the sugar completely dissolves.
   - Bring to a boil, then remove from heat and let it cool slightly.
2. Make the sorbet:
   - Place the sumac in a heat-resistant container.
   - Pour the hot syrup over the sumac.
   - Stir well to combine.
3. Chill and serve:
   - Allow the mixture to cool to room temperature.
   - Refrigerate until chilled.
   - Stir before serving.
   - Serve cold.

- Sumakh (sumac) is a tart, burgundy-colored spice common in Middle Eastern, Armenian and Azerbaijani cuisine.
- This drink is a unique way to enjoy sumac, transforming the spice into a refreshing beverage.

Apricot Compote

 6 servings   1 hour

INGREDIENTS

- 2 cups dried apricots
- 4 cups water
- 1 cup sugar
- 1 cinnamon stick
- 4-5 cardamom pods

DIRECTIONS

1. In a pot, combine dried apricots, water, sugar, cinnamon stick, and cardamom pods.
2. Bring the mixture to a boil, then reduce the heat and simmer for about 20-25 minutes until the apricots are tender.
3. Allow the compote to cool, then refrigerate.
4. Serve chilled and enjoy the sweet and spiced flavors

T'tu Lavash (Armenian Sour Fruit Rollups)

 6 servings   1 hour

INGREDIENTS

- 2 lbs (900g) sour plums, pitted (or a mix of sour plums and apricots)
- 1/4 cup (60ml) honey (optional, for balancing sourness)
- 1 tsp lemon juice
- Equipment:
- Food processor or blender
- Fine-mesh strainer or cheesecloth
- Dehydrator or oven
- Parchment paper

- Store in an airtight container at room temperature for up to 1 month, or refrigerate for longer storage.
- The sourness level can be adjusted by the type and ripeness of plums used. For a more intense sour flavor, use unripe plums. For a milder taste, include some ripe apricots in the mix

DIRECTIONS

1. Wash and pit the plums, remove pits as well.
2. Place fruit in a food processor until smooth.
3. Pour the puree through a fine-mesh strainer or cheesecloth to remove any bits of skin or fibers.
4. If desired, mix in honey to balance sourness. Add lemon juice to help preserve color.
5. Line dehydrator trays or baking sheets with parchment paper.
6. Spread the puree evenly in thin layers, about 1/8 inch thick.
7. If using a dehydrator: Set to 135°F (57°C) and dry for 6-8 hours, or until the fruit is leathery but still pliable.
8. If using an oven: Set to lowest temperature (usually around 170°F/75°C). Prop the door open slightly with a wooden spoon. Dry for 6-8 hours, checking regularly.
9. The lavash is ready when it's no longer sticky to the touch but still flexible.
10. Allow to cool completely at room temperature.
11. Carefully peel off the parchment paper.
12. Roll up the fruit leather tightly.

Pakhlava

🍴 8 servings   🕐 50 min

INGREDIENTS

For the pastry:
- 500g phyllo dough sheets
- 250g unsalted butter, melted

For the filling:
- 500g walnuts, finely chopped
- 100g sugar
- 1 tsp ground cardamom

For the syrup:
- 2 cups sugar
- 1 cup water
- 1 tbsp lemon juice
- 1 tsp rose water (optional)

- Pakhlava is a rich, sweet pastry popular throughout the Middle East and Caucasus.
- In Azerbaijan, it's especially associated with Novruz celebrations in March.
- The diamond shape is traditional for Azerbaijani pakhlava.
- Walnuts are the most common nut used in Azerbaijani versions, but other nuts can be used.

DIRECTIONS

1. Prepare the filling:
   - Mix chopped walnuts, sugar, and cardamom in a bowl.
2. Assemble the pakhlava:
   - Preheat oven to 180°C (350°F).
   - Brush a baking pan with melted butter.
   - Layer 8-10 sheets of phyllo dough, brushing each with melted butter.
   - Spread 1/3 of the nut mixture evenly over the dough.
   - Repeat the process two more times, ending with a layer of buttered phyllo sheets on top.
3. Cut and bake:
   - Cut the pakhlava into diamond shapes.
   - Bake for 45-50 minutes, until golden brown and crisp.
4. Make the syrup:
   - While the pakhlava is baking, combine sugar and water in a saucepan.
   - Bring to a boil, then simmer for 10 minutes.
   - Remove from heat, add lemon juice and rose water if using.
5. Finish the pakhlava:
   - Remove pakhlava from the oven and immediately pour the hot syrup over it.
   - Let it cool completely to absorb the syrup.

Armenian Ponchik (Filled Doughnuts)

🍴 8 servings 🕐 50 min

INGREDIENTS

For the dough:
- 3 cups all-purpose flour
- 1/4 cup sugar
- 2 1/4 tsp (1 packet) active dry yeast
- 1/2 tsp salt
- 1 cup warm milk
- 2 eggs, beaten
- 1/4 cup unsalted butter, melted
- 1 tsp vanilla extract

For frying:
- Vegetable oil for deep frying

For the fillings (choose one or both): Chocolate filling:
- 1 cup semi-sweet chocolate chips
- 1/4 cup heavy cream

Vanilla cream filling:
- 1 cup milk
- 1/4 cup sugar
- 2 egg yolks
- 2 tbsp cornstarch
- 1 tsp vanilla extract

For dusting:
- 1/2 cup powdered sugar

DIRECTIONS

Prepare the dough:
1. In a large bowl, mix flour, sugar, yeast, and salt.
2. Add warm milk, beaten eggs, melted butter, and vanilla. Mix until a soft dough forms.
3. Knead for 5-7 minutes until smooth and elastic.
4. Place in a greased bowl, cover, and let rise in a warm place for 1 hour or until doubled.
5. Prepare fillings: For chocolate: Melt chocolate chips with heavy cream in a double boiler. Cool slightly. For vanilla cream: Whisk milk, sugar, egg yolks, and cornstarch in a saucepan. Cook over medium heat, stirring constantly, until thickened. Add vanilla and cool completely.

Shape and fill:
1. Punch down dough and roll out to 1/4 inch thickness.
2. Cut into 3-inch circles.
3. Place a spoonful of filling in the center of each circle.
4. Fold edges over filling and pinch to seal completely.

Fry the ponchiks:
1. Heat oil to 350°F (175°C) in a deep fryer or heavy pot.
2. Fry ponchiks in batches for 2-3 minutes per side until golden brown.
3. Drain on paper towels.

Finish and serve:
1. While still warm, dust ponchiks generously with powdered sugar.
2. Serve immediately for the best experience.

Syunik-Vayots Dzor Region

Boreks (Spinach and Cheese Turnovers)

 10 servings   1.5 hrs

INGREDIENTS

- 10 oz frozen spinach, thawed and squeezed dry
- 1 cup crumbled feta cheese
- 1/2 cup shredded Muenster or Monterey Jack cheese
- 1/4 cup cottage cheese or cream cheese
- 2 eggs, lightly beaten
- 1/4 cup chopped fresh parsley
- 2 scallions, finely chopped
- 1 tbsp fresh dill, chopped
- Salt and pepper to taste

For assembly:
- 1 package (16 oz) phyllo dough, thawed
- 1/2 cup unsalted butter, melted
- Sesame seeds for garnish (optional)

DIRECTIONS

1. Preheat oven to 375°F (190°C).
2. Mix all filling ingredients in a large bowl until well combined.
3. Lay out one sheet of phyllo dough and brush lightly with melted butter. Place another sheet on top and brush with butter again.
4. Cut the phyllo into 3-inch wide strips.
5. Place a tablespoon of filling at one end of each strip.
6. Fold the corner of the phyllo over the filling to form a triangle. Continue folding the strip in a triangle pattern until you reach the end.
7. Place the borek on a baking sheet lined with parchment paper. Brush the top with melted butter and sprinkle with sesame seeds if using.
8. Repeat with remaining phyllo and filling.
9. Bake for 20-25 minutes, or until golden brown and crispy.
10. Let cool for a few minutes before serving.

These boreks can be served warm or at room temperature as part of a mezze spread or as a standalone appetizer. The combination of crispy phyllo and savory, cheesy spinach filling makes for a delicious and satisfying treat. Remember to keep the unused phyllo covered with a damp towel while working to prevent it from drying out.

Meat Roulade in Puff Pastry

 10 servings   1 hr

INGREDIENTS

- 1/2 lb (250g) ground beef
- 1/2 lb (250g) ground pork
- 2 eggs (1 for mixture, 1 for egg wash)
- 1 medium onion, grated
- 1/2 cup (50g) breadcrumbs
- 1/4 cup (30g) grated Parmesan cheese
- 1/3 cup (80g) sun-dried tomatoes, chopped
- 1/2 tsp dried basil
- 1 tsp salt
- 1/4 tsp ground black pepper
- 1 sheet (250g) puff pastry, thawed
- 1 tbsp sesame seeds for topping

Note: You can customize the filling by adding different herbs or cheeses to suit your taste.
CopyRetry

DIRECTIONS

1. Preheat oven to 350°F (180°C). Line a baking sheet with parchment paper.
2. In a large bowl, combine ground beef, pork, 1 egg, grated onion, breadcrumbs, Parmesan, sun-dried tomatoes, basil, salt, and pepper. Mix well.
3. Shape the mixture into a log, about 2 inches in diameter.
4. Roll out the puff pastry on a lightly floured surface. Place the meat log in the center.
5. Fold the pastry over the meat, sealing the edges. Place seam-side down on the prepared baking sheet.
6. Make diagonal slashes across the top of the pastry. Beat the remaining egg and brush over the pastry. Sprinkle with sesame seeds.
7. Bake for 35-40 minutes, until the pastry is golden brown and the meat is cooked through (internal temperature should reach 160°F/71°C).
8. Let rest for 5 minutes before slicing and serving hot

Serving Suggestion: This elegant roulade is perfect for holiday dinners or special occasions. Serve with a side salad or roasted vegetables for a complete meal.

Oven-Roasted Chicken Kebabs

 10 servings 1 hr

INGREDIENTS

- 2 large chicken breasts, cut into 1-inch cubes
- 1 cup buttermilk (or kefir)
- 2 medium onions, sliced into rings
- 4 medium tomatoes, grated (discard skins)
- Salt to taste
- Black pepper to taste
- 1 tbsp poultry seasoning (or a mix of dried herbs like thyme, rosemary, and oregano)
- Wooden skewers, soaked in water for 30 minutes

Note: If you don't have buttermilk, you can make a quick substitute by adding 1 tablespoon of lemon juice or white vinegar to 1 cup of milk and letting it sit for 5 minutes before using.

DIRECTIONS

1. In a large bowl, combine chicken cubes, buttermilk, onion rings, grated tomatoes, salt, pepper, and poultry seasoning. Mix well to coat chicken. Marinate for at least 30 minutes or up to 2 hours in the refrigerator.
2. Preheat oven to 375°F (190-200°C). Line a baking sheet with parchment paper.
3. Thread marinated chicken pieces onto skewers, alternating with onion rings.
4. Arrange skewers on the prepared baking sheet, leaving space between each.
5. Roast for 30-40 minutes, turning once halfway through, until chicken is golden brown and cooked through (internal temperature should reach 165°F/74°C).
6. Let rest for 5 minutes before serving.

Serving Suggestion: Serve these juicy chicken kebabs with a side of roasted vegetables or a fresh salad. They're perfect for a family dinner or casual entertaining.

Oven-Baked Potato and Eggplant Casserole

 10 servings   2 hr

INGREDIENTS

- 2.2 lbs (1 kg) potatoes
- 1 lb (500 g) eggplant
- 1 lb (500 g) tomatoes
- 5 tablespoons sour cream
- 2 cloves garlic, minced
- 3.5 oz (100 g) cheese, grated
- Vegetable oil, as needed
- Salt and pepper to taste

Note: For a richer flavor, you can add layers of sautéed onions or bell peppers between the vegetables. You can also customize the cheese according to your preference - mozzarella or cheddar work well in this dish.

DIRECTIONS

1. Slice eggplant into rounds. Sprinkle with salt and let sit for 20 minutes. Rinse and pat dry.
2. In a skillet, fry eggplant slices in oil until golden. Set aside.
3. Boil potatoes for 25-30 minutes until just tender. Cool slightly, then slice into rounds.
4. Slice tomatoes into rounds.
5. Preheat oven to 350°F (180°C).
6. Mix sour cream with minced garlic.
7. Grease a baking dish. Layer ingredients as follows:
8. Potato slices (season with salt and pepper, spread with some sour cream mixture)
9. Eggplant slices (season, spread with sour cream mixture)
10. Tomato slices (season with salt)
11. Top with grated cheese.
12. Cover with foil and bake for 1 hour.
13. Remove foil and bake for an additional 10-15 minutes until cheese is golden and bubbly.
14. Serve hot.

Serving Suggestion: This hearty vegetable casserole makes a great side dish or vegetarian main course. It pairs well with grilled meats or can be enjoyed on its own with a fresh salad.

Tomato Paste Perlotto (Pearl Barley Risotto)

🍴 10 servings 🕐 40 min

INGREDIENTS

- 1 cup pearl barley
- 14 oz (400g) fresh tomatoes
- 2 tablespoons tomato paste
- 1 medium onion, finely chopped
- 3 cloves garlic, minced
- Sugar to taste
- Salt to taste
- 1 sprig fresh rosemary, leaves chopped
- 1 sprig fresh basil, leaves torn
- Ground black pepper to taste
- 2 tablespoons olive oil

Serving Suggestion: This hearty perlotto makes a great vegetarian main dish or a side for grilled meats. It's a nutritious alternative to traditional risotto, with a delightful chewy texture from the pearl barley.

DIRECTIONS

1. Soak pearl barley overnight in water. Drain and rinse.
2. In a pot, cover barley with fresh water and simmer for 15-20 minutes until tender but still firm. Drain and set aside.
3. While barley cooks, heat olive oil in a large skillet over medium heat. Add onion and garlic, sauté until softened.
4. Peel and crush tomatoes with a fork. Add to the skillet along with tomato paste, salt, and sugar to taste. Stir well.
5. Add chopped rosemary and torn basil leaves. Simmer for 10 minutes.
6. Add cooked pearl barley to the tomato mixture. Stir and simmer for another 5 minutes to allow flavors to meld.
7. Season with black pepper to taste.
8. Serve hot, garnished with fresh herbs if desired.

Sour Cream Chicken Bake

 10 servings   40 min

INGREDIENTS

- For the filling:
- 12 oz (360g) boneless chicken, diced
- 1 medium onion, sliced
- 1 tbsp fresh ginger, minced
- 2 cloves garlic, minced
- 2 tbsp vegetable oil
- 2 tbsp soy sauce
- Salt and black pepper to taste
- 2 tbsp fresh parsley, chopped
- For the batter:
- 1 1/2 cups (360g) sour cream
- 2 large eggs
- 3/4 cup (200g) mayonnaise
- 3/4 cup (100g) all-purpose flour
- 1/2 tsp baking soda
- Pinch of salt

Note: You can adjust the amount of ginger to suit your taste. For a spicier version, add a pinch of cayenne pepper to the chicken mixture.

DIRECTIONS

1. Preheat oven to 350°F (180°C). Grease a 9-inch pie dish.
2. In a large skillet, heat oil over high heat. Add chicken and cook for 30 seconds.
3. Add onions and cook until chicken is browned and onions are softened.
4. Remove from heat. Stir in ginger, garlic, soy sauce, salt, pepper, and parsley. Set aside.
5. In a large bowl, whisk together eggs, sour cream, mayonnaise, baking soda, and salt.
6. Gradually stir in flour until you have a smooth batter.
7. Pour half the batter into the prepared pie dish.
8. Spread the chicken mixture over the batter.
9. Pour the remaining batter over the chicken, spreading to cover completely.
10. Bake for 30 minutes, or until the top is golden brown and a toothpick inserted in the center comes out clean.
11. Let cool for 5 minutes before serving.

Serving Suggestion: This savory bake is delicious served warm as a main course with a side salad. The combination of sour cream batter and ginger-infused chicken creates a unique and flavorful dish.

Kanachi plate

🍴 10 servings   🕐 5 min

INGREDIENTS

Kanachi plate, also known as "kanachi poodnos" in Armenian, is a traditional appetizer or mezze platter in Armenian cuisine. "Kanachi" means "green" in Armenian, and this platter typically features a variety of fresh green vegetables and herbs

The kanachi plate is typically served as part of a larger spread of appetizers or as a side dish to main meals. It's especially popular during spring and summer when fresh herbs and vegetables are abundant.

To eat from a kanachi plate, diners typically pick up the herbs and vegetables with their hands, sometimes dipping them in salt or olive oil. The fresh, crisp vegetables and aromatic herbs are meant to cleanse the palate

DIRECTIONS

Fresh herbs:
- Tarragon (tarkhun)
- Cilantro
- Parsley
- Basil
- Green onions
- Dill

Green vegetables:
- Cucumbers, sliced or whole
- Green bell peppers, sliced
- Green chilies (optional)
- Other items often included:
- Radishes
- Green unripe plums (when in season)
- Green onions with roots intact
- Young garlic shoots

Accompaniments:
- Salt for sprinkling on vegetables
- Sometimes a small bowl of olive oil for dipping

Parsley and Onion Omelette

 1 serving   25 minutes

INGREDIENTS

- 6 large eggs
- 4-5 medium onions, finely chopped
- 1/4 cup vegetable oil or butter
- 1/2 cup fresh herbs (mix of parsley, cilantro, dill, and/or green onions), finely chopped
- 1 tsp turmeric (optional, but traditional)
- Salt and black pepper to taste
- Flatbread for serving

DIRECTIONS

1. Prepare the onions:
   - Heat half the oil in a large non-stick skillet over medium heat.
   - Add the chopped onions and cook until soft and golden, about 15-20 minutes.
   - Remove from heat and let cool slightly.
2. Make the egg mixture:
   - In a large bowl, beat the eggs.
   - Add the cooled onions, chopped herbs, turmeric (if using), salt, and pepper.
   - Mix well to combine all ingredients.
3. Cook the eggs:
   - Heat the remaining oil in the same skillet over medium heat.
   - Pour in the egg mixture, spreading it evenly.
   - Cook for about 5-7 minutes, or until the bottom is set and golden brown.
4. Finish cooking:
   - Place a large plate over the skillet and carefully invert the eggs onto the plate.
   - Slide the eggs back into the skillet, uncooked side down.
   - Cook for another 3-5 minutes, until fully set and golden on both sides.
5. Serve:
   - Slide the onto a serving plate.
   - Cut into wedges and serve hot or at room temperature with flatbread.

Fat Fried Liver

🍴 4 servings   🕐 55 minutes

INGREDIENTS

- 1 lb beef or lamb liver, thinly sliced
- 1 tablespoon mutton fat (rendered from sheep tail fat or obtained from a butcher)
- 1 small onion, thinly sliced
- Salt, to taste

DIRECTIONS

1. Heat the mutton fat in a large skillet or frying pan over medium heat until melted and hot.
2. Add the thinly sliced onion to the skillet and sauté until softened and translucent, about 3-4 minutes.
3. Push the onions to one side of the skillet and add the thinly sliced liver to the other side. Cook the liver for 2-3 minutes on each side, or until browned and cooked through.
4. Once the liver is cooked, mix it with the onions and continue cooking for another minute.
5. Reduce the heat to low and add the tail fat to the skillet. Cook it over low heat until it starts to render its fat slightly.
6. Mix the rendered tail fat with the liver and onions, and continue cooking for another 1-2 minutes, stirring occasionally.
7. Season the liver and onions with salt, to taste, and stir to combine.
8. Remove the skillet from heat and transfer the tail fat fried liver to a serving platter.
9. Serve hot and enjoy

Roast Chicken with Rice, Apricot, and Chestnut Stuffing

4 servings   55 minutes

INGREDIENTS

- 1 whole chicken (about 4-5 lbs)
- 1 cup long-grain rice
- 1/2 cup dried apricots, chopped
- 1/2 cup cooked chestnuts, roughly chopped
- 1 onion, finely diced
- 2 cloves garlic, minced
- 1/4 cup butter
- 1/4 cup chopped fresh parsley
- 1 tsp dried thyme
- 1/2 tsp ground cinnamon
- Salt and pepper to taste
- 2 tbsp olive oil

For the glaze:
- 2 tbsp apricot jam
- 1 tbsp lemon juice
-

DIRECTIONS

Prepare the Stuffing:
1. Cook rice according to package instructions. Set aside to cool.
2. In a large skillet, melt butter over medium heat. Sauté onion until translucent.
3. Add garlic, cook for another minute.
4. Stir in chopped apricots, chestnuts, parsley, thyme, and cinnamon.
5. Combine with cooled rice. Season with salt and pepper.

Stuff and Prepare the Chicken:
1. Preheat oven to 375°F (190°C).
2. Rinse chicken and pat dry. Season cavity with salt and pepper.
3. Loosely fill the cavity with the stuffing mixture.
4. Tie legs together with kitchen twine and tuck wing tips under.
5. Rub chicken skin with olive oil, salt, and pepper.

Roast the Chicken:
1. Place chicken breast-side up in a roasting pan.
2. Roast for about 1 hour and 30 minutes, or until juices run clear when thigh is pierced.

Glaze the Chicken:
1. Mix apricot jam with lemon juice.
2. During the last 15 minutes of roasting, brush chicken with glaze.
3. Rest and Serve:
4. Let chicken rest for 10-15 minutes before carving.
5. Serve with extra stuffing on the side.

Note: Ensure the internal temperature of both chicken and stuffing reaches 165°F (74°C) for food safety.

Lentil Soup

 4 servings   55 minutes

INGREDIENTS

- 1/4 tsp cinnamon
- 1 tsp paprika
- 1/4 tsp red or cayenne pepper
- 1 1/2 tsp salt
- 1 tbsp dried mint
- 2 tbsp olive oil
- 3 medium celery stalks, chopped
- 1 medium eggplant (about 10 oz), cubed
- 3 tbsp fresh parsley, chopped
- 7 1/2 cups water
- 1 medium bell pepper, chopped
- 2.8 oz dried apricots, chopped
- 14.5 oz can finely chopped tomatoes
- 1 cup yellow lentils

DIRECTIONS

1. Rinse lentils. Bring to a boil in water and simmer for 20 minutes. Add chopped apricots and celery, simmer for another 20 minutes.
2. Meanwhile, sauté chopped bell pepper in oil for a few minutes. Add cubed eggplant and cook until almost tender. Add dried spices, salt, and tomatoes. Cover and cook until tender, about 10 minutes.
3. Stir sautéed vegetables into the lentil-apricot mixture and simmer for 15 minutes. Add chopped fresh parsley and mint.
4. Serve with dark bread and sharp cheese if desired.

Note: Each serving is about 1 1/2 cups.
This recipe yields a hearty, flavorful soup that combines the earthiness of lentils with the sweetness of apricots and the richness of vegetables. It's a perfect example of Armenian cuisine's balance of flavors and textures.

Stuffed eggplant

🍴 6 servings 🕐 75 minutes

INGREDIENTS

- 2 large eggplants
- 1/4 cup olive oil, divided
- 1 small onion, finely chopped
- 2 cloves garlic, minced
- 2 medium tomatoes, diced
- 2 tablespoons tomato paste
- 1/2 teaspoon sugar
- 1/2 teaspoon dried oregano
- 1/4 teaspoon ground cumin
- Salt and pepper to taste
- 2 tablespoons fresh parsley, chopped
- Lemon wedges for serving

DIRECTIONS

1. In a small bowl, dissolve the yeast in lukewarm milk and let it sit for 5 Preheat the oven to 180°C (350°F).
2. Slice the eggplants in half lengthwise, leaving the stems intact. Score the cut sides of the eggplants with a knife in a crisscross pattern.
3. Place the eggplant halves on a baking sheet and brush the cut sides with 2 tablespoons of olive oil. Bake in the preheated oven for about 25 minutes or until the flesh becomes soft and tender.
4. While the eggplants are baking, heat the remaining 2 tablespoons of olive oil in a skillet over medium heat.
5. Add the chopped onion and minced garlic to the skillet and sauté until they become translucent and fragrant.
6. Stir in the diced tomatoes, tomato paste, sugar, dried oregano, ground cumin, salt, and pepper. Cook the mixture for about 5 minutes, allowing the flavors to blend and the tomatoes to soften.
7. Remove the eggplants from the oven and let them cool slightly. Use a spoon to carefully scoop out the flesh from the center of each eggplant half, leaving about a 1/4-inch thick shell.
8. Chop the scooped-out eggplant flesh into small pieces and add it to the skillet with the tomato mixture. Stir well to combine.
9. Fill the hollowed-out eggplant shells with the tomato and eggplant mixture, pressing it down gently with the back of a spoon.
10. Return the stuffed eggplants to the oven and bake for an additional 15-20 minutes, or until the tops are slightly browned.
11. Remove the Imam Bayildi from the oven and let it cool for a few minutes.
12. Garnish with fresh parsley and serve warm or at room temperature with lemon wedges on the side.

Sour Cream Salad

🍴 1 serving   🕐 25 minutes

INGREDIENTS

- 60g tomatoes
- 45g cucumbers
- 15g fresh green onions
- 20g regular onion
- 40g radishes
- 30g sour cream
- 10g fresh dill
- Salt and pepper to taste
- Green lettuce leaves for garnish

DIRECTIONS

1. Prepare the vegetables:
   - Slice tomatoes, cucumbers, and radishes into thin circles.
   - Cut the regular onion into rings.
   - Finely chop the green onions and dill.
2. Assemble the salad:
   - Arrange the sliced tomatoes, cucumbers, and radishes on a plate.
   - Place the chopped green onions in the center of the plate.
   - Arrange the onion rings on top of the tomatoes.
3. Season and dress:
   - Sprinkle salt and pepper over the vegetables.
   - Drizzle sour cream over the salad.
4. Garnish:
   - Sprinkle finely chopped dill over the entire salad.
   - Arrange green lettuce leaves around the edges of the plate.

Tanabour

 4 servings   55 minutes

INGREDIENTS

- 4 cups plain yogurt (preferably Armenian or Greek)
- 4 cups water
- 1/2 cup bulgur wheat (fine grain)
- 1 egg, beaten
- 2 tablespoons all-purpose flour
- 2 tablespoons butter
- 1 small onion, finely chopped
- 2 cloves garlic, minced
- 1/4 cup fresh mint, chopped (or 2 tablespoons dried mint)
- Salt to taste
- Dried mint for garnish
-

DIRECTIONS

1. In a large pot, whisk together the yogurt, water, and beaten egg until smooth.
2. Gradually whisk in the flour to avoid lumps.
3. Add the bulgur wheat and a pinch of salt. Bring the mixture to a gentle simmer over medium heat, stirring constantly.
4. Reduce heat to low and let it simmer for about 15-20 minutes, stirring frequently, until the bulgur is tender and the soup has thickened slightly.
5. In a separate small pan, melt the butter over medium heat. Add the chopped onion and garlic, sautéing until the onion is translucent and fragrant.
6. Add the sautéed onion and garlic mixture to the soup, along with the fresh or dried mint.
7. Simmer for an additional 5 minutes, stirring occasionally.
8. Taste and adjust salt as needed.
9. Serve hot, garnished with a sprinkle of dried mint on top.

Tanabour is typically served as a starter or light main course. The yogurt gives the soup a creamy, tangy flavor, while the bulgur adds texture and body. The mint provides a fresh, aromatic note that complements the yogurt beautifully.

Targhana Soup

 4 servings   55 minutes

INGREDIENTS

- 1 cup targhana (dried fermented grain product, can be found in Middle Eastern stores)
- 6 cups chicken or vegetable broth
- 1 onion, finely chopped
- 2 tablespoons butter or olive oil
- 1 tablespoon tomato paste
- 1 teaspoon paprika
- Salt and pepper to taste
- 1 tablespoon dried mint (optional)
- Plain yogurt for serving (optional)

DIRECTIONS

1. Soak the targhana in 2 cups of warm water for about 30 minutes.
2. In a large pot, heat the butter or oil over medium heat. Add the chopped onion and sauté until translucent, about 5 minutes.
3. Add the tomato paste and paprika to the onions and cook for another minute, stirring constantly.
4. Drain the soaked targhana and add it to the pot. Stir to coat with the onion mixture.
5. Pour in the broth and bring to a boil. Reduce heat and simmer for about 15-20 minutes, or until the targhana is tender and the soup has thickened.
6. Season with salt and pepper to taste.
7. If using, stir in the dried mint just before serving.
8. Serve hot, with a dollop of yogurt if desired.

Note: The consistency of the soup can vary depending on personal preference. If it's too thick, you can add more broth or water. If it's too thin, let it simmer for a few more minutes to reduce.

Stuffed Grape Leaves

 8 servings   50 min

INGREDIENTS

- 1 jar of grape leaves (about 50-60 leaves)
- 500g ground lamb (or beef)
- 1 cup short-grain rice, rinsed
- 1 large onion, finely chopped
- 1/4 cup butter, melted
- 1/4 cup each of fresh coriander, dill, and mint, finely chopped
- 1 tsp salt
- 1/2 tsp black pepper
- 2 cups water or broth

For serving:
- Plain yogurt
- Lemon wedges

- Using high-quality, tender grape leaves is crucial for the best taste and texture.

DIRECTIONS

1. Prepare the grape leaves:
   - If using jarred leaves, rinse them gently to remove excess brine.
   - Blanch fresh leaves in boiling water for 1-2 minutes, then cool in ice water.
2. Prepare the filling:
   - In a large bowl, mix ground lamb, rice, chopped onion, melted butter, herbs, salt, and pepper.
   - Mix well until all ingredients are evenly combined.
3. Stuff the leaves:
   - Lay a grape leaf flat, vein-side up, on your work surface.
   - Place about 1 tablespoon of filling near the stem end of the leaf.
   - Fold the sides over the filling, then roll tightly from the stem end.
   - Repeat with remaining leaves and filling.
4. Cook the dolma:
   - Line the bottom of a large pot with any torn or unused grape leaves.
   - Arrange the stuffed leaves in tight, neat layers in the pot.
   - Pour 2 cups of water or broth over the dolma.
   - Place a heat-proof plate on top to keep the rolls submerged.
   - Cover the pot and bring to a simmer.
   - Cook on low heat for about 45-50 minutes, until the rice is tender.
5. Serve:
   - Allow to cool slightly before serving.
   - Arrange on a platter and serve warm or at room temperature.
   - Accompany with plain yogurt and lemon wedges.

Roasted Red Pepper and Tomato Spread

 10 servings   60 minutes

INGREDIENTS

- 4 large red bell peppers
- 4 ripe tomatoes
- 2 medium onions, finely chopped
- 4 cloves garlic, minced
- 2 tablespoons olive oil
- 2 tablespoons red wine vinegar
- 1 teaspoon sugar
- 1 teaspoon salt
- 1/2 teaspoon ground black pepper
- Fresh parsley or cilantro, chopped (for garnish)

DIRECTIONS

1. Preheat your oven to the broil setting. Line a baking sheet with aluminum foil.
2. Place the red bell peppers and tomatoes on the baking sheet. Broil for about 15-20 minutes, turning occasionally, until the skin of the peppers and tomatoes is charred and blistered.
3. Remove the baking sheet from the oven and transfer the peppers and tomatoes to a heatproof bowl. Cover the bowl with plastic wrap and let them cool for about 15 minutes. This will help loosen the skin.
4. Once cooled, peel off the skin of the peppers and tomatoes. Remove the stems and seeds from the peppers. Dice the peppers and tomatoes into small pieces.
5. In a large skillet, heat the olive oil over medium heat. Add the chopped onions and minced garlic. Sauté for about 5-7 minutes, until the onions are translucent and fragrant.
6. Add the diced peppers and tomatoes to the skillet. Stir in the red wine vinegar, sugar, salt, and black pepper. Mix well to combine.
7. Reduce the heat to low and let the mixture simmer for about 30-40 minutes, stirring occasionally. This will allow the flavors to meld together and the mixture to thicken.
8. Remove the skillet from the heat and let the pindjur cool to room temperature.

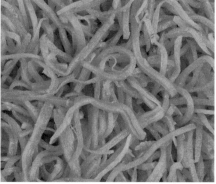

Carrot Salad with Yogurt Dressing

 10 servings 30 minutes

INGREDIENTS

For the Salad:

- 4 cups shredded carrots
- 1/2 cup raisins
- 1/2 cup chopped nuts (walnuts or almonds)
- 1/4 cup fresh cilantro, chopped
- 1/4 cup fresh mint, chopped

For the Yogurt Dressing:

- 1 cup plain yogurt
- 2 tablespoons olive oil
- 1 tablespoon honey
- 2 cloves garlic, minced
- 1 teaspoon ground cumin
- 1 teaspoon ground coriander
- Salt and pepper to taste

DIRECTIONS

For the Salad:

1. Peel and shred the carrots using a grater or food processor.
2. In a large bowl, combine the shredded carrots, raisins, chopped nuts, fresh cilantro, and fresh mint. Toss gently to mix the ingredients evenly.

For the Yogurt Dressing:

1. In a separate bowl, whisk together the plain yogurt, olive oil, honey, minced garlic, ground cumin, ground coriander, salt, and pepper. Ensure a smooth and well-incorporated dressing.
2. Pour the yogurt dressing over the carrot mixture. Toss the salad gently to ensure that all ingredients are coated with the flavorful dressing.
3. Taste the salad and adjust the seasoning with salt and pepper if needed.
4. Transfer the Samarkand Carrot Salad to a serving dish.
5. This refreshing salad is a perfect accompaniment to grilled meats or enjoyed on its own.

Crescent Cookies

🍴 10 servings 🕐 45 min

INGREDIENTS

- 3 cups all-purpose flour
- 1 cup unsalted butter, softened
- 1 cup powdered sugar
- 2 eggs
- 1 tsp vanilla extract
- 1/2 tsp baking powder
- Pinch of salt
- Extra sugar for sprinkling

DIRECTIONS

:

1. Cream butter and sugar until light and fluffy.
2. Beat in eggs and vanilla extract.
3. Gradually mix in flour, baking powder, and salt to form a soft dough.
4. Chill the dough for about an hour.
5. Shape the dough into desired forms (circles, crescents, etc.).
6. Brush with egg wash and sprinkle with sugar.
7. Bake until golden brown.

Cultural Significance:

1. Shaker-churek is often prepared for holidays, particularly Novruz (New Year) celebrations.
2. It's a popular treat to offer guests, symbolizing hospitality.
3. The sweet bread is sometimes used in traditional ceremonies or rituals.

Variations:

1. Some recipes may include nuts, such as walnuts or almonds.

Delicious Coconut Cookies

 10 servings   35 min

INGREDIENTS

- 2.5 cups unsweetened finely shredded coconut
- 2/3 cup sweetened condensed milk
- 1/2 teaspoon vanilla extract
- 2 egg whites
- 1/4 teaspoon salt

DIRECTIONS

1. In a bowl, combine the shredded coconut.
2. Pour in the condensed milk, add vanilla extract, and mix well.
3. In another bowl, beat the egg whites with salt until stiff peaks form.
4. Gently fold the beaten egg whites into the coconut mixture.
5. Use a spoon to shape the mixture into small balls and place them on a baking sheet lined with parchment paper.
6. Bake in a preheated oven at 325°F (160°C) for about 25 minutes or until lightly golden.
7. Allow the cookies to cool on the baking sheet for a few minutes before transferring them to a wire rack to cool completely.

Gata (Armenian Sweet Pastry)

 8 servings 50 min

INGREDIENTS

For the dough:
- 2¼ sticks (1 cup + 2 tbsp) salted butter
- 1 cup sour cream
- 1 large egg
- 1 tsp baking powder
- 3-3½ cups all-purpose flour

For the filling:
- 10 tbsp melted salted butter
- 1 cup granulated sugar
- 1 tsp vanilla extract
- 1½ cups flour
- 2 cups finely chopped walnuts
- 1 cup chopped dates
- ⅔ cup chopped dried apricots
- ⅔ cup chopped dried prunes
- 1 cup raisins (mixed gold and black)

For brushing:
- 1 egg white (for brushing dough before filling)
- 1 egg yolk (for egg wash)

DIRECTIONS

1. Make dough: In a large bowl, mix butter, sour cream, and egg. Combine baking powder with 3 cups flour, then gradually add to wet ingredients. Mix until soft dough forms, adding more flour if needed. Refrigerate 30 minutes.
2. Prepare filling: Whisk melted butter, sugar, and vanilla. Stir in flour, then fold in nuts and dried fruits.
3. Preheat oven to 375°F. Line baking sheet with parchment.
4. Roll dough on floured surface into 18x24 inch rectangle, about ¼ inch thick.
5. Brush entire dough surface with egg white.
6. Spread filling evenly, leaving 1-inch border around edges.
7. Tightly roll dough from long side, pinching seam to seal.
8. Transfer to baking sheet, seam-side down. Shape into circle or leave as log.
9. Brush top and sides with egg yolk for golden finish.
10. Bake 30-35 minutes until golden brown. Cover with foil if browning too quickly.
11. Cool on baking sheet 10 minutes, then transfer to wire rack to cool completely.
12. Slice into 1-inch pieces when fully cooled for cleaner cuts.

Baked Pumpkin

🍴 2 servings   🕐 35 minutes

INGREDIENTS

- 4 cups pumpkin, peeled and diced
- 1 cup sugar
- 1/2 cup water
- 1/2 cup walnuts, chopped
- 1/4 cup raisins
- 1 teaspoon ground cinnamon
- 1/2 teaspoon ground cardamom
- 1/4 teaspoon ground cloves
- 1/4 teaspoon salt
- 2 tablespoons butter
- Greek yogurt or whipped cream for serving (optional)

DIRECTIONS

1. Peel and dice the pumpkin into small, bite-sized pieces.
2. In a large pot, combine the diced pumpkin, sugar, and water. Bring to a simmer over medium heat and cook until the pumpkin is tender but still holds its shape.
3. Stir in chopped walnuts, raisins, ground cinnamon, ground cardamom, ground cloves, and salt. Mix well to ensure the spices are evenly distributed.
4. Allow the mixture to simmer over low heat for an additional 10 minutes, allowing the flavors to meld and the pumpkin to absorb the spices.
5. Stir in butter until melted, giving the dessert a rich and velvety texture.
6. Can be served warm or at room temperature. Optionally, serve it with a dollop of Greek yogurt or a swirl of whipped cream for added richness.

Blueberry pannacota

🍴 10 servings 🕐 1 hrs

INGREDIENTS

- 2 teaspoons gelatin
- 1 teaspoon gelatin
- 3/4 cup heavy cream
- 1/4 cup sugar
- 3/4 cup milk
- 1 teaspoon vanilla extract
- 3/4 cup water
- 3 tablespoons sugar
- Juice of half a lemon
- 1 1/2 cups fresh blueberries
- Food coloring
- Fresh mint leaves for garnish

DIRECTIONS

1. **Preparing Gelatin**: Start by dividing the gelatin into two separate bowls - 2 teaspoons in one bowl and 1 teaspoon in the other. Add cold water to each bowl. Stir and let it stand for 7-10 minutes until softened.

2. **Preparing Cream Mixture**: In a saucepan, mix 3/4 cup heavy cream, 1/4 cup sugar, and 3/4 cup milk. Place the saucepan over low heat. Dissolve the sugar in the mixture. Add 1 teaspoon vanilla extract.

3. **Mixing Gelatin**: Take the bowl with 2 teaspoons of gelatin. Stir well with the cream mixture until completely dissolved. Place this mixture in the refrigerator for 1 hour to set.

4. **Preparing Blueberry Sauce**: In another saucepan, mix 3/4 cup water, 3 tablespoons sugar, and juice of half a lemon. Heat the mixture over medium heat. Dissolve the sugar completely. Add 1 teaspoon gelatin from the second bowl. Stir until the gelatin dissolves. Add food coloring to achieve the desired shade.

5. **Adding Blueberries**: Gently fold 1 1/2 cups of fresh blueberries into the blueberry sauce. Let the mixture cool.

6. **Assembly**: Remove the gelatin and cream mixture from the refrigerator. Pour the blueberry sauce over the cream mixture in molds.

7. **Chilling Time**: Place the molds in the refrigerator for about 30 minutes until the panna cotta sets completely.

Honey Sesame Candy

🍴 4 servings   🕐 60 minutes

INGREDIENTS

- 1 cup sesame seeds
- 1/2 cup honey
- 1/4 cup unsalted butter
- 1/2 cup chopped nuts (pistachios, almonds, or walnuts), optional
- 1/2 teaspoon vanilla extract
- Pinch of salt

DIRECTIONS

1. Toast the sesame seeds in a dry skillet over medium heat until they turn golden brown. Keep a close eye on them and stir frequently to prevent burning.
2. In a saucepan, combine honey, unsalted butter, and a pinch of salt. Heat over medium-low heat, stirring continuously until the butter is melted and the mixture is well combined.
3. Allow the honey-butter mixture to simmer gently for about 5-7 minutes, stirring occasionally. The syrup should thicken slightly.
4. Add the toasted sesame seeds and chopped nuts (if using) to the syrup. Continue stirring to coat the seeds and nuts evenly.
5. Remove the saucepan from heat and stir in the vanilla extract, ensuring it's well incorporated.
6. While the mixture is still warm, transfer it to a parchment-lined dish or tray. Use a spatula to spread it evenly, creating a smooth surface.
7. Allow the mixture to cool at room temperature for a while, and then refrigerate until fully set. Once set, use a sharp knife to cut the candy into small squares or rectangles.

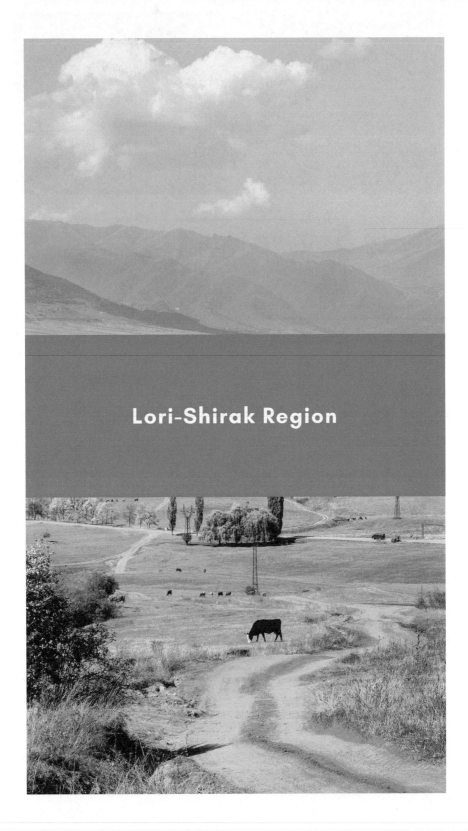

Lori-Shirak Region

Gelorig Meatball Soup

🍴 10 servings   🕐 55 minutes

INGREDIENTS

For the meatballs (kufta):

- 500g ground lamb or beef
- 1 small onion, finely grated
- 1/4 cup rice, soaked and drained
- 1 egg
- Salt and pepper to taste

For the soup:

- 2 tablespoons vegetable oil
- 1 large onion, chopped
- 2 medium potatoes, cubed
- 1 cup peas (fresh or frozen)
- 500g mutton bones (optional, for extra flavor)
- 8 cups water or beef broth
- 2 tablespoons tomato paste
- 1 teaspoon turmeric
- Salt and pepper to taste
- 6-8 dried plums (optional)
- Fresh herbs (cilantro or parsley) for garnish

- The addition of mutton bones enriches the broth's flavor.

DIRECTIONS

1. Prepare the meatballs:
   - Mix ground meat, grated onion, rice, egg, salt, and pepper.
   - Form into large meatballs (about 6-8).
2. Start the soup:
   - Heat oil in a large pot. Sauté chopped onion until golden.
   - Add mutton bones (if using) and water or broth. Bring to a boil.
   - Reduce heat and simmer for 30 minutes.
3. Cook the meatballs:
   - Gently add the meatballs to the simmering broth.
   - Cook for about 20 minutes.
4. Add vegetables and seasonings:
   - Add cubed potatoes, peas, tomato paste, and turmeric.
   - Simmer for another 15-20 minutes until potatoes are tender.
5. Finish the soup:
   - Add dried plums if using.
   - Season with salt and pepper to taste.
   - Simmer for an additional 5 minutes.
6. Serve:
   - Ladle soup into bowls, ensuring each serving has a large meatball.
   - Garnish with fresh herbs.

Zhingalov Khats
Herb-Filled Flatbread

 10 servings 55 minutes

INGREDIENTS

- 2 1/2 oz leeks, thinly sliced
- 2 1/2 oz scallions (white and green parts), thinly sliced
- 2 oz unsalted butter
- 3/4 oz flat-leaf parsley, finely chopped
- 1 recipe lavash dough
- Olive oil for cooking
- All-purpose flour for rolling

Using a wok is a way to substitute for a clay oven, which none of us have a home. If you don't have that, you can put the flatbread in a well oil heated pan instead.

DIRECTIONS

1. Prepare the Filling: In a small saucepan, melt butter over medium heat. Add leeks and scallions, cooking until soft. Remove from heat and let cool. Stir in chopped parsley.
2. Shape the Dough: Divide lavash dough into 4 equal portions. On a well-floured surface, roll each portion into a 10" x 12" oval, giving quarter turns between rolls to maintain shape.
3. Fill and Reshape: Spread leek mixture evenly over each oval. Fold sides over and re-roll to original size, adding flour as needed to prevent sticking.

Cook the Flatbreads:

1. Invert a wok over high heat on a gas burner. Heat for several minutes.
2. Lightly oil the wok surface with olive oil using a paper towel.
3. Place one flatbread on the wok. Cook for about 1 minute, then flip. Continue cooking and flipping every minute until browned and cooked through.
4. Serve: Eat immediately for best taste and texture. If serving later, cover with a towel and spritz with water before reheating.

Note: For optimal results, cook each flatbread just before serving.

Khashlama

🍴 10 servings   🕐 55 minutes

INGREDIENTS

- 2 lbs bone-in lamb chops (or beef if preferred)
- 3 large tomatoes, sliced
- 2 bell peppers, sliced
- 2 large onions, sliced
- 6 cloves of garlic, whole
- 2 medium potatoes, sliced
- 2 carrots, sliced
- 1 bunch fresh parsley
- Salt and black pepper to taste
- 1 tsp dried thyme
- 2 bay leaves

Note: This dish is all about slow cooking to develop flavors. Be patient and let it simmer gently. Each family might have their own preferred spices or additional vegetables, so feel free to adjust to your taste.

DIRECTIONS

1. In a large, heavy-bottomed pot, begin layering the ingredients:
2. Start with a layer of sliced onions
3. Add a layer of meat
4. Follow with layers of tomatoes, bell peppers, potatoes, and carrots
5. Sprinkle each layer with salt, pepper, and a pinch of thyme
6. Repeat the layering process until all ingredients are used
7. Add the whole garlic cloves, bay leaves, and half the parsley between layers.
8. Do not add water - the ingredients will release their own juices.
9. Cover the pot with a tight-fitting lid.
10. Place over low heat and cook for about 2-3 hours. Do not stir.
11. Check occasionally, tasting the broth to adjust seasoning if needed.
12. The dish is ready when the meat is very tender and falling off the bone.
13. Garnish with the remaining fresh parsley before serving.
14. Serve hot with lavash bread or rice.

Armenian Kelekyosh (Lentil and Yogurt Soup)

 10 servings   40 minutes

INGREDIENTS

- 2 1/4 cups (1 lb) dried lentils
- 1 lb onions, finely chopped
- 2 tablespoons vegetable oil
- 4 cups (32 oz) plain yogurt
- 1 large egg
- 1 tablespoon all-purpose flour
- 1 teaspoon dried thyme
- 1 teaspoon dried mint
- 4 oz dried lavash bread, broken into small pieces
- Salt to taste

Note: Kelekyosh is traditionally served during festive occasions. It can be enjoyed on its own or with additional pieces of lavash bread for dipping. The layering technique allows diners to experience all flavors in each spoonful.

DIRECTIONS

1. In a large pot, cook lentils in 6 cups of water until very soft and mushy, about 30-40 minutes. Drain any excess water.
2. In a skillet, heat oil over medium heat. Add onions and cook until golden brown, about 10-15 minutes. Stir in thyme and mint during the last minute of cooking.
3. In a separate saucepan, whisk together yogurt, egg, and flour. Cook over medium-low heat, stirring constantly, until the mixture thickens slightly, about 5-7 minutes. Be careful not to let it boil.
4. In a large serving bowl, layer ingredients as follows:
5. Half of the broken lavash pieces
6. Half of the cooked lentils
7. Half of the yogurt mixture
8. Half of the onion mixture Repeat layers with remaining ingredients.
9. Gently stir to combine all ingredients. Season with salt to taste.
10. Serve warm, garnished with additional dried herbs if desired.

Crispy Cabbage Cutlets

 12 servings　 40 minutes

INGREDIENTS

- 2 lbs (1 kg) cabbage, quartered
- 1 medium onion, finely chopped
- 1/4 cup fresh dill, chopped
- 2 cloves garlic, minced
- 1/2 cup all-purpose flour
- 1/2 cup wheat flour
- 1 cup breadcrumbs
- 1/2 cup vegetable oil for frying
- Salt and black pepper to taste

Serve hot with your favorite sauce, a side of mixed greens, or steamed vegetables. These cutlets pair particularly well with tomato sauce or garlic aioli.

Note: For a variation, try substituting cauliflower for the cabbage. These vegetarian cutlets are perfect for Lent or as a meatless option any time of year.

DIRECTIONS

1. Bring a large pot of salted water to a boil. Add cabbage quarters and cook for 5 minutes. Drain in a colander and let cool slightly.
2. In a food processor, pulse each cabbage quarter separately until finely chopped.
3. In a large bowl, combine chopped cabbage, onion, dill, and garlic. Season with salt and pepper.
4. Add both flours to the cabbage mixture and mix well. Let stand for 5-7 minutes to allow the flour to absorb moisture.
5. Shape the mixture into 12 patties, about 1/2 inch thick.
6. Place breadcrumbs in a shallow dish. Coat each patty in breadcrumbs.
7. Heat oil in a large skillet over medium-high heat.
8. Fry cutlets in batches for 3-4 minutes per side, or until golden brown and crispy.
9. Drain on paper towels.

Basterma with Eggs

 2 servings 15 min

INGREDIENTS

- 4 oz (about 120g) basterma, thinly sliced
- 4 large eggs
- 2 tablespoons butter or olive oil
- 1/4 teaspoon black pepper
- 1/4 cup chopped fresh parsley (optional)
- Lavash or pita bread for serving

DIRECTIONS

1. Heat a large non-stick skillet over medium heat. Add 1 tablespoon of butter or oil.
2. Once the butter has melted or the oil is hot, add the sliced basterma to the pan. Cook for about 1-2 minutes per side, just until it starts to crisp slightly. Be careful not to overcook as basterma is already cured and dried.
3. Remove the basterma from the pan and set aside.
4. In the same pan, add the remaining butter or oil.
5. Crack the eggs directly into the pan. Cook sunny-side up or to your preferred doneness.
6. As the eggs are cooking, sprinkle them with black pepper.
7. Just before the eggs are done to your liking, return the basterma to the pan, placing it around and between the eggs to reheat slightly.
8. Remove from heat and sprinkle with chopped parsley if using.
9. Serve immediately with warm lavash or pita bread.

Note: Some variations of this dish involve scrambling the eggs with chopped basterma. If you prefer this method, chop the basterma and add it to beaten eggs before cooking them together in the pan.

Open-Faced Meat Pie with Potato Crust

🍴 2 servings   🕐 1 hr

INGREDIENTS

For the crust:

- 1 large or 2 medium potatoes (about 7 oz/200g)
- 1 cup all-purpose flour
- 1 egg
- 3 1/2 tablespoons (50g) butter
- Salt to taste

For the filling:

- 14 oz (400g) ground meat (beef or pork)
- 1 medium onion, finely chopped
- 1 1/2 cups (150-200g) cauliflower, chopped
- 2 eggs
- 3 tablespoons sour cream
- 2 medium tomatoes, sliced
- 1/2 cup grated cheese
- Salt to taste
- Vegetable oil for sautéing

Serving Suggestion: This hearty pie is perfect for a family dinner. Serve with a fresh green salad on the side.

DIRECTIONS

1. Preheat oven to 400°F (200°C).

For the crust:

1. Boil potatoes until tender. Drain and mash.
2. Mix mashed potatoes with butter, egg, and salt.
3. Gradually add flour to form a soft dough.
4. Roll out to fit a 9-inch pie dish.

For the filling:

1. Sauté cauliflower for 5 minutes, add a bit of water, cover and cook for 5 more minutes.
2. In another pan, sauté onion and ground meat until browned.
3. Combine cauliflower and meat mixture.

Assemble the pie:

1. Place potato crust in a greased pie dish.
2. Spread meat and vegetable mixture over crust.
3. Whisk 2 eggs with sour cream and pour over filling.
4. Top with sliced tomatoes and grated cheese.
5. Bake for 40 minutes or until crust is golden and filling is set.
6. Let cool for 5 minutes before slicing and serving.

Kerusous (Armenian One-Pot Meal)

 2 servings   40 min

INGREDIENTS

- 1 lb (450g) beef, cut into 1-inch cubes
- 2 large potatoes, peeled and cubed
- 1 cup green beans, trimmed and cut into 1-inch pieces
- 1 bell pepper, chopped
- 2 medium tomatoes, diced
- 1 onion, chopped
- 1 cup peas (fresh or frozen)
- 1-2 chili peppers, finely chopped (adjust to taste)
- 1 cup mixed greens (such as spinach, parsley, and dill), chopped
- 3 tbsp vegetable oil
- 2 cloves garlic, minced
- 1 tsp paprika
- Salt and black pepper to taste
- Water as needed

DIRECTIONS

1. Heat 2 tbsp oil in a large skillet or pot over medium-high heat.
2. Add beef cubes and brown on all sides, about 5-7 minutes. Remove and set aside.
3. Sauté the vegetables:
4. In the same pot, add remaining oil if needed.
5. Add onions and garlic, sauté until translucent, about 3 minutes.
6. Add potatoes and cook for 5 minutes, stirring occasionally.
7. Return beef to the pot.
8. Add green beans, bell pepper, tomatoes, peas, and chili peppers.
9. Stir in paprika, salt, and black pepper.
10. Add about 1/2 cup of water, or enough to barely cover the ingredients.
11. Bring to a boil, then reduce heat to low.
12. Cover and simmer for about 30-40 minutes, or until beef and potatoes are tender.
13. Finish the dish:
14. Stir in the mixed greens and cook for an additional 5 minutes.
15. Taste and adjust seasoning if needed.
16. Serve hot, directly from the pot.

Lamb Stew with Tarragon

4 servings   30 minutes

INGREDIENTS

- 1.5 lbs (700g) lamb or beef, cut into chunks
- 2 bunches of tarragon
- 1 bunch of cilantro
- 1 bunch of parsley
- 1 bunch of mint
- 1 large onion, finely chopped
- 4 cloves garlic, minced
- 2 cups white wine
- 1 cup water
- 2 tablespoons white wine vinegar
- 4 tablespoons olive oil
- Salt and pepper to taste

DIRECTIONS

1. **Prepare Herbs:**
   - Wash and finely chop tarragon, cilantro, parsley, and mint.
2. **Brown Meat:**
   - In a large pot, heat olive oil over medium heat. Add lamb/beef chunks, and brown them on all sides.
3. **Add Onion and Garlic:**
   - Add chopped onion and minced garlic. Sauté until onions are translucent.
4. **Pour Wine and Vinegar:**
   - Pour in white wine and white wine vinegar. Let it simmer briefly to reduce the alcohol.
5. **Add Water and Season:**
   - Add water to the pot, season with salt and pepper, and bring to a gentle simmer.
6. **Incorporate Herbs:**
   - Stir in chopped tarragon, cilantro, parsley, and mint. Ensure everything is well combined.
7. **Simmer:**
   - Cover the pot and simmer over low to medium heat for 1.5 to 2 hours until the meat is tender.
8. **Adjust Seasoning:**
   - Taste and adjust seasoning if necessary.

Cheesy Breadsticks

🍴 10 servings   🕐 1 hour

INGREDIENTS

- 1 1/3 cups (170g) all-purpose flour
- 1 cup (150g) grated cheese (such as cheddar or Parmesan)
- 7 tablespoons (100g) unsalted butter, softened
- 1/3 cup (100ml) milk
- 1/4 teaspoon salt
- 1/3 teaspoon baking powder
- Zest of 1/2 lemon
- 1 tablespoon sesame seeds

Note: These breadsticks will be slightly soft when first out of the oven but will become crispy after cooling for a few hours. Store in an airtight container to maintain crispness.

DIRECTIONS

1. In a large bowl, mix softened butter, grated cheese, lemon zest, and salt until well combined.
2. Stir in the milk.
3. In a separate bowl, whisk together flour and baking powder.
4. Gradually add the flour mixture to the cheese mixture, stirring until a dough forms.
5. Knead the dough briefly, then wrap in plastic wrap and refrigerate for 30 minutes.
6. Preheat oven to 350°F (180°C). Line a baking sheet with parchment paper.
7. On a floured surface, roll out the dough to a rectangle about 12 inches wide and 1/4 inch thick.
8. Trim the edges to make a neat rectangle, then cut into strips about 1/2 inch wide.
9. Twist each strip gently, then roll in sesame seeds.
10. Place the twists on the prepared baking sheet.
11. Bake for 15-20 minutes, until golden brown.
12. Allow to cool on the baking sheet.

Tomato and Bulgur Soup

🍴 10 servings 🕐 25 minutes

INGREDIENTS

- 3 cups vegetable stock
- 1 cup onions, chopped finely
- 1 cup carrots, diced
- ¾ cup celery, diced (2 med stalks)
- 2 large garlic cloves, crushed
- 1 tsp salt
- 1 tsp dried dill
- ½ tsp ground fennel
- 1 tin undrained tinned tomatoes, chopped

¼ cup raw bulgur wheat

DIRECTIONS

1. In large soup pot, combine stock, onions, celery, garlic, salt, dill and fennel.

2. Bring to boil, reduce heat, cover and simmer gently for 5 minutes.

3. Stir in tomatoes and juice.

4. Add bulgur and mix well.

5. Return to boil and simmer, covered, for another 15 minutes or until bulgur is tender. Stir occasionally. If using cooked quinoa, just heat it through and give it a stir.

6. Add pepper to taste.

7. Serve with crusty bread – or hot garlic bread.

Tabbouleh

 10 servings 20 min

INGREDIENTS

- 1/2 cup fine bulgur wheat
- 2 cups very finely chopped fresh parsley (about 2 large bunches)
- 1/2 cup finely chopped fresh mint
- 1/4 cup finely chopped onion
- 2 medium tomatoes, diced small
- 1/4 cup extra virgin olive oil
- 1/4 cup freshly squeezed lemon juice
- 1/2 teaspoon salt
- 1/4 teaspoon black pepper
- Romaine lettuce leaves for serving (optional)

DIRECTIONS

1. Rinse the bulgur wheat and soak it in cold water for about 30 minutes. Drain well and squeeze out excess water.
2. In a large bowl, combine the soaked bulgur, chopped parsley, mint, onion, and tomatoes.
3. In a small bowl, whisk together the olive oil, lemon juice, salt, and pepper.
4. Pour the dressing over the bulgur mixture and toss gently to combine.
5. Cover and refrigerate for at least an hour to allow the flavors to meld.
6. Before serving, taste and adjust seasoning if needed.
7. Serve chilled or at room temperature, optionally in romaine lettuce leaves as wraps.

Tabbouleh is traditionally a parsley-heavy salad, with bulgur wheat playing a supporting role. The key is to chop the parsley very finely. This salad is refreshing, light, and packed with flavor. It's often served as part of a mezze spread or as a side dish to grilled meats. In Armenian cuisine, it might be served alongside other Middle Eastern-influenced dishes like hummus, falafel, or grilled kebabs.

Spanakhov Asoudi

🍴 10 servings   🕐 20 min

INGREDIENTS

- 1 lb fresh spinach, washed and chopped
- 2 cups plain Greek yogurt
- 2 cloves garlic, minced
- 2 tablespoons olive oil
- 1 small onion, finely chopped
- 1/2 teaspoon salt (or to taste)
- 1/4 teaspoon black pepper
- 1/4 cup chopped walnuts (optional)
- 1 tablespoon lemon juice (optional)

DIRECTIONS

1. In a large pot, bring water to a boil. Add the chopped spinach and cook for 2-3 minutes until wilted.
2. Drain the spinach well and squeeze out excess water. Let it cool.
3. In a large bowl, mix the Greek yogurt with minced garlic, salt, and pepper.
4. Heat olive oil in a pan over medium heat. Add the chopped onion and sauté until translucent and slightly golden.
5. Add the cooled spinach to the pan with onions and stir for 1-2 minutes to combine flavors.
6. Remove from heat and let the spinach mixture cool to room temperature.
7. Fold the spinach and onion mixture into the garlic yogurt.
8. If using, stir in the chopped walnuts and lemon juice.
9. Taste and adjust seasoning if needed.
10. Cover and refrigerate for at least an hour to allow flavors to meld.
11. Serve chilled or at room temperature.

This salad is a refreshing and healthy dish that combines the earthiness of spinach with the tangy creaminess of yogurt. It's often served as part of a mezze spread or as a side dish. The walnuts add a nice crunch and the lemon juice brightens the flavors. In Armenian cuisine, this type of yogurt-based salad is popular and variations may include other vegetables or herbs.

Pasuts Tolma

 10 servings 1 hr

INGREDIENTS

- 900g (1 large jar) pickled cabbage leaves, washed and drained
- 2 cans (15 oz each) red kidney beans (or pinto/white beans)
- 1 can (16-18 oz) lentils
- 1 can (15 oz) chickpeas
- 3/4 cup fine bulgur (#1 grind)
- 1 large onion, finely chopped or minced
- 5-7 tbsp extra virgin olive oil
- 1 tbsp tomato paste
- 1 tbsp red pepper paste
- 1/2 tsp ground black pepper
- 1 tsp paprika
- 1/2 tsp cayenne or red chili flakes (optional)
- 1/2 tsp ground coriander
- 2-3 tsp dried herbs (dill, basil, thyme)
- 3-4 tbsp fresh herbs (dill, cilantro, parsley), chopped
- 1 tsp salt
- 6-8 dried sour plums or prunes (optional)
- 1 1/2 - 2 cups boiling water

DIRECTIONS

1. In a large bowl, combine the drained beans, lentils, chickpeas, and fine bulgur.
2. In a pan, sauté the finely chopped onion in olive oil until translucent.
3. Add tomato paste and red pepper paste to the onions, cook for 2-3 minutes.
4. Add the onion mixture to the bean and bulgur mixture.
5. Stir in all the spices, dried herbs, fresh herbs, and salt.
6. Pour in the boiling hot water, mix well, and let stand for 15-20 minutes until the bulgur softens.
7. Carefully separate and lay out the pickled cabbage leaves.
8. Place a spoonful of the filling in the center of each leaf and roll tightly, tucking in the sides.
9. Arrange the rolled tolma in a large pot or deep pan.
10. If using, place dried sour plums or prunes between the rolls.
11. Pour any remaining liquid from the filling over the rolls.
12. Cover the pot and cook on low heat for about 45 minutes to 1 hour, until the cabbage is tender and the filling is heated through.
13. Allow to cool, then refrigerate for several hours or overnight before serving.

This cold appetizer is perfect for make-ahead holiday meals and tastes even better the next day. It's a flavorful, vegetarian dish that's popular during Armenian New Year celebrations.

Baked Zucchini Halves

🍴 10 servings 🕐 55 minutes

INGREDIENTS

- 3 zucchinis
- 14 oz mixed ground meat
- 1 carrot
- 7 oz cheese
- 2 tbsp sweet chili sauce
- 3 cloves of garlic
- Salt to taste

DIRECTIONS

1. **Prepare the zucchinis:**
   - Wash the zucchinis and cut them lengthwise in half. Scoop out the insides to form boats.
2. **Prepare the zucchini boats:**
   - Rub each boat with a generous amount of grated garlic and sprinkle with a little salt.
3. **Prepare the filling:**
   - Peel and grate the carrot, then cook it.
   - After a while, add the chopped zucchini pulp, cut into small pieces. Cook for a few minutes.
   - Then add the ground meat and cook until it's lightly pink.
   - Add curls, salt to taste, and a few tablespoons of sweet chili sauce.
4. **Stuff the zucchini boats:**
   - Fill the zucchini boats with the prepared mixture.
5. **Bake:**
   - Cover with foil and bake at 200°C (390°F) for 25 minutes.
   - Remove the foil, sprinkle with cheese, and bake until it's lightly browned.

Pomegranate Seeds Pilaf

 6 servings   55 minutes

INGREDIENTS

For the pilaf:

- 1 kg rice
- 2 whole chickens (500g each)
- 7-8 onions, finely chopped
- 150g raisins
- 150g dried apricots, chopped
- 100g pomegranate seeds
- 100g chestnuts, cooked and peeled
- 1/2 tsp salt
- 2 pinches black pepper

For the gazmakh (crispy bottom layer):

- 1 cup wheat flour
- 2 tsp vegetable oil
- 40g sour cream
- 40g katyk (natural yogurt)
- 20g sugar
- Pinch of salt

- Nardancha Pilaf is named after its distinctive use of pomegranate seeds (nardancha).

DIRECTIONS

1. Prepare the chicken:
   - Clean and cut the chickens into pieces.
   - Season with salt and pepper, then brown in a large pot.
   - Add water to cover and simmer until tender.
2. Prepare the rice:
   - Rinse the rice until water runs clear.
   - Par-boil in salted water for 5-7 minutes, then drain.
3. Make the gazmakh:
   - Mix all gazmakh ingredients to form a batter.
   - Spread thinly on the bottom of a large, heavy-bottomed pot.
4. Assemble the pilaf:
   - Layer half the rice over the gazmakh.
   - Add the chicken pieces, chopped dried fruits, and chestnuts.
   - Cover with the remaining rice.
   - Pour in some of the chicken broth.
5. Cook the pilaf:
   - Make holes in the rice with a wooden spoon handle for steam to escape.
   - Cover with a lid wrapped in a kitchen towel.
   - Cook on low heat for about 30-40 minutes.
6. Serve:
   - Gently mix the layers.
   - Garnish with pomegranate seeds.

Roast Goose with Apricots in Wine

 6 servings 3 hrs

INGREDIENTS

- 1 whole goose (10-12 lbs), giblets removed
- 1 lb dried apricots
- 2 cups dry white wine
- 1 large onion, quartered
- 2 apples, quartered
- 4 cloves garlic, crushed
- 2 tbsp olive oil
- 1 tbsp salt
- 1 tsp black pepper
- 1 tsp dried thyme
- 1 cinnamon stick

For the glaze:

- 1/4 cup honey
- 2 tbsp lemon juice

Note: Save rendered goose fat for future cooking - it's excellent for roasting potatoes.

DIRECTIONS

1. Preheat oven to 375°F (190°C).
2. Rinse goose inside and out, pat dry.
3. Prick skin all over with a fork
4. Rub inside and outside with olive oil, salt, pepper, and thyme.
5. Place onion quarters, apple quarters, and crushed garlic inside the cavity. Set aside for now.
6. In a saucepan, combine dried apricots, white wine, and cinnamon stick.
7. Bring to a boil, then simmer for 10 minutes. Remove from heat and set aside.
8. Place goose breast-side up on a rack in a roasting pan.
9. Roast for 2 hours, basting every 30 minutes with pan juices.
10. After 2 hours, remove goose from oven. Drain apricots, reserving the wine.
11. Scatter apricots around the goose in the roasting pan.
12. Pour 1 cup of the reserved wine over the goose and apricots.
13. Return to oven and roast for another 30-45 minutes, or until skin is golden and crisp, and internal temperature reaches 165°F (74°C) at the thickest part of the thigh.
14. Prepare Glaze: Mix honey and lemon juice.
15. During the last 15 minutes of roasting, brush goose with glaze.
16. Let goose rest for 20 minutes before carving.
17. Serve sliced goose with roasted apricots and pan juices.

Pamidorov Dzvadzegh (Creamy Armenian Scrambled Eggs with Tomatoes)

 4 servings   30 min

INGREDIENTS

- 4 large eggs
- 2 medium ripe tomatoes, diced
- 1 small onion, finely chopped
- 2 tablespoons butter or olive oil
- 1/4 cup heavy cream
- 1/4 cup fresh parsley, finely chopped (plus extra for garnish)
- Salt and pepper to taste
- 1/4 teaspoon dried oregano (optional)

The addition of cream will make the eggs richer and more luxurious, while the extra parsley will enhance the fresh, herbaceous flavors in the dish.

DIRECTIONS

- Heat butter or oil in a large skillet over medium heat.
- Add the chopped onion and sauté until translucent, about 3-4 minutes.
- Add the diced tomatoes to the skillet. Cook for about 5 minutes, stirring occasionally, until the tomatoes start to break down and release their juices.
- In a bowl, beat the eggs with salt, pepper, and heavy cream.
- Stir in 1/4 cup of chopped fresh parsley to the egg mixture.
- Pour the egg mixture into the skillet with the tomato mixture.
- Reduce heat to low and gently stir the eggs as they cook, creating soft curds.
- Cook until the eggs are just set but still slightly creamy, about 3-4 minutes.
- If using, sprinkle with dried oregano.
- Remove from heat and garnish with additional chopped fresh parsley.
- Serve immediately with fresh bread or lavash.

Fruit Compote

 10 servings   10 minutes

INGREDIENTS

- 1 cup dried fruit mix (such as apples, apricots, plums, cherries)
- 4 cups water
- 1 cinnamon stick
- 4-5 whole cloves
- 1 tablespoon honey or sugar (optional)
- Lemon or orange zest (optional)

DIRECTIONS

1. Place the dried fruit mix in a large pot and add water, cinnamon stick, and whole cloves.
2. If desired, add a tablespoon of honey or sugar to sweeten the compote. You can adjust the sweetness to your preference.
3. Optional: Add some lemon or orange zest for extra flavor. This step is purely optional but can add a refreshing citrus note to the compote.
4. Bring the mixture to a boil over medium-high heat, then reduce the heat to low and let it simmer for about 30-40 minutes. Stir occasionally.
5. Once the fruit has softened and absorbed the flavors of the spices, remove the pot from the heat.
6. Allow to cool to room temperature before serving, or you can refrigerate it for a few hours to serve it chilled.
7. Serve in bowls, including some of the liquid with the fruit.

Sweet sujuk

Candy

 7 servings   🕐 55 minutes

INGREDIENTS

- 2 cups of walnuts (or almonds, hazelnuts, or a mix), shelled
- 1 cup of flour (all-purpose or wheat)
- 1 cup of sugar
- 1 teaspoon of ground cinnamon (optional)
- 1 teaspoon of vanilla extract (optional)
- 2 cups of grape juice (ideally, freshly squeezed)
- 1 cup of water
- Cotton thread for stringing

DIRECTIONS

1. **Prepare the Nuts:**
   - If your nuts are not already shelled, crack and peel them. You can use a variety of nuts or a combination based on your preference.
2. **String the Nuts:**
   - Thread the nuts onto a piece of cotton thread, creating a string of nuts. Make sure the nuts are close together, forming a dense line.
3. **Make the Flour Mixture:**
   - In a mixing bowl, combine the flour, sugar, and ground cinnamon (if using). Mix well. You can also add vanilla extract for extra flavor.
4. **Dip Nuts in Flour Mixture:**
   - Dip the nut strings into the flour mixture, ensuring that the nuts are evenly coated. This will help the grape juice mixture adhere to the nuts.
5. **Prepare the Grape Juice Mixture:**
   - In a separate bowl, mix the grape juice and water. This will be the liquid mixture for coating the nut strings.
6. **Dip in Grape Juice Mixture:**
   - Dip the flour-coated nut strings into the grape juice mixture, ensuring they are fully coated. Allow any excess liquid to drip off.
7. **Repeat the Process:**
   - Repeat the process of dipping the nut strings into the flour mixture and then the grape juice mixture at least 4-5 times. This layering process will create a thick coating.
8. **Hang to Dry:**
   - Hang the coated nut strings in a cool, dry place for several days until the churchkhela is completely dry and firm.
9. **Slice and Serve:**
   - Once the Sweet sujuk is dry, use a sharp knife to slice it into bite-sized pieces. The result is a delicious, chewy, and sweet treat.

Honey Cookies

🍴 2 servings 🕐 50 minutes

INGREDIENTS

- 1 3/4 cups all-purpose flour
- 1/2 cup unsalted butter, softened
- 1/2 cup granulated sugar
- 2 tablespoons honey
- 1 large egg
- 1 teaspoon baking powder
- 1/2 teaspoon ground cinnamon (optional)
- Pinch of salt
- Powdered sugar for dusting (optional)

DIRECTIONS

1. **Preheat the Oven:**
   1. Preheat your oven to 350°F (175°C). Line a baking sheet with parchment paper or lightly grease it.
2. **Prepare the Dough:**
   1. In a mixing bowl, cream together the softened butter and granulated sugar until light and fluffy.
   2. Add the egg and honey, and mix until well combined.
3. **Combine Dry Ingredients:**
   1. In a separate bowl, whisk together the all-purpose flour, baking powder, ground cinnamon (if using), and a pinch of salt.
4. **Mix the Dough:**
   1. Gradually add the dry ingredients to the wet ingredients, mixing until a smooth dough forms. If the dough is too sticky, you can add a little more flour.
5. **Shape the Cookies:**
   1. Roll out the dough on a lightly floured surface to about 1/4 inch thickness. Use cookie cutters to cut out shapes or simply shape the dough into small balls and flatten them slightly.
6. **Bake the Cookies:**
   1. Place the cookies on the prepared baking sheet, leaving some space between each cookie.
   2. Bake in the preheated oven for 10-12 minutes, or until the cookies are golden brown around the edges.
7. **Cool and Dust:**
   1. Allow the cookies to cool on the baking sheet for a few minutes before transferring them to a wire rack to cool completely.
   2. Once cooled, you can dust the cookies with powdered sugar if desired.

Honey Cake

🍴 10 servings   🕐 25 minutes

INGREDIENTS

For the Cake:

- 2 cups all-purpose flour
- 1 teaspoon baking powder
- 1/2 teaspoon baking soda
- 1/2 teaspoon salt
- 1 teaspoon ground cinnamon
- 1/2 teaspoon ground cloves
- 1/2 cup unsalted butter, softened
- 1/2 cup granulated sugar
- 1/2 cup honey
- 3 large eggs
- 1 teaspoon vanilla extract
- 1 cup buttermilk

For the Honey Glaze:

- 1/4 cup unsalted butter
- 1/4 cup honey
- 1/4 cup brown sugar
- 1/4 cup heavy cream
- 1/2 teaspoon vanilla extract
- Chopped nuts for garnish (optional)

DIRECTIONS

1. **Preheat the Oven:**
   - Preheat your oven to 350°F (180°C). Grease and flour a cake pan.
2. **Make the Cake:**
   - In a bowl, whisk together the flour, baking powder, baking soda, salt, cinnamon, and ground cloves. Set aside.
   - In another large bowl, cream together the softened butter and granulated sugar until light and fluffy.
   - Add the honey, eggs (one at a time), and vanilla extract. Mix well after each addition.
   - Gradually add the dry ingredients to the wet ingredients, alternating with the buttermilk. Begin and end with the dry ingredients. Mix until just combined.
   - Pour the batter into the prepared cake pan and smooth the top.
3. **Bake the Cake:**
   - Bake in the preheated oven for 25-30 minutes or until a toothpick inserted into the center comes out clean.
   - Allow the cake to cool in the pan for 10 minutes before transferring it to a wire rack to cool completely.
4. **Make the Honey Glaze:**
   - In a small saucepan, combine the butter, honey, brown sugar, and heavy cream. Cook over medium heat, stirring constantly, until the mixture comes to a boil.
   - Remove from heat and stir in the vanilla extract. Let the glaze cool for a few minutes.
5. **Glaze the Cake:**
   - Place the cooled cake on a serving platter. Pour the honey glaze over the cake, allowing it to drizzle down the sides.
   - Optionally, garnish the top of the cake with chopped nuts.
6. **Serve:**
   - Allow the glaze to set before slicing and serving.

Crumb cake

 10 servings   1 hrs

INGREDIENTS

For the Crust & Topping:

- 2 cups (250g) all-purpose flour
- 1 cup (125g) whole wheat or spelt flour
- 1/2 cup (100g) granulated sugar
- 1/2 tsp salt
- 1 cup (225g) cold unsalted butter, cubed
- 1 large egg

For the Filling:

- 2 cups (500g) thick jam or fruit preserves (any flavor)

DIRECTIONS

1. Preheat oven to 400°F (200°C). Grease a 9x13 inch baking pan and line with parchment paper, leaving an overhang on two sides.
2. In a large bowl, whisk together the all-purpose flour, whole wheat flour, sugar and salt. Cut in the cold butter using a pastry blender or two forks until mixture resembles coarse crumbs.
3. Transfer 1 cup of the crumb mixture to a separate bowl and set aside for the topping.
4. To the remaining crumb mixture, add the egg and mix with a fork until a soft dough forms.
5. Press the dough evenly into the prepared baking pan to form a crust. Spread the jam evenly over the crust.
6. Top with the reserved crumb topping, squeezing some crumbs together to create larger clumps.
7. Bake for 30-35 minutes, until the topping is lightly golden brown.
8. Allow to cool completely in the pan on a wire rack before cutting into bars.

Variations:

- Add 1/2 cup sweetened shredded coconut or chopped nuts to the crumb topping
- Use any flavor jam or preserves like strawberry, raspberry, apricot or lingonberry

C

 10 servings 1 hrs

INGREDIENTS

- 1 cup (125g) all-purpose flour
- 2 tablespoons caster sugar
- 1/2 teaspoon baking soda
- Pinch of salt
- 1 cup (240ml) milk
- 1 large egg
- 1 teaspoon vanilla extract
- Butter or lard for greasing the pan
- Assorted fruits (e.g., raspberries, sliced bananas, chunks of mango)
- Maple syrup or honey for drizzling
- Whipped cream for topping (optional)

DIRECTIONS

1. **Prepare the Batter:**
   - In a mixing bowl, combine the flour, caster sugar, baking soda, and a pinch of salt.
2. **Combine Wet Ingredients:**
   - In a separate bowl, whisk together the milk, egg, and vanilla extract.
3. **Mix Dry and Wet Ingredients:**
   - Gradually pour the wet ingredients into the dry ingredients, stirring continuously to avoid lumps. Mix until you have a smooth batter.
4. **Rest the Batter:**
   - Allow the batter to rest for about 15-20 minutes. This helps the flour absorb the liquid and results in fluffier pancakes.
5. **Heat the Pan:**
   - Heat a non-stick frying pan or griddle over medium heat. Add a small amount of butter or lard to coat the surface.
6. **Cook the Pancakes:**
   - Pour a ladleful of batter onto the hot pan, swirling it to spread the batter evenly. Cook until bubbles form on the surface, then flip and cook the other side until golden brown.
7. **Prepare Fruits:**
   - Wash and prepare the assortment of fruits. Berries can be used whole, and other fruits can be sliced or diced.
8. **Assemble:**
   - Place a stack of pancakes on a plate. Top with the assorted fruits.
9. **Drizzle and Top:**
   - Drizzle maple syrup or honey over the pancakes and fruits. Optionally, top with whipped cream for an extra indulgence.